Adventuring WITH KIDS

YOSEMITE
NATIONAL PARK

HARLEY AND ABBY MCALLISTER

MOUNTAINEERS
BOOKS

MOUNTAINEERS BOOKS is dedicated to the exploration, preservation, and enjoyment of outdoor and wilderness areas.

1001 SW Klickitat Way, Suite 201 • Seattle, WA 98134
800-553-4453 • www.mountaineersbooks.org

Printed in China
Distributed in the United Kingdom by Cordee, www.cordee.co.uk
First edition, 2019

Copyeditor: Emily Dings
Design: Heidi Smets
Layout: McKenzie Long
Cartographer: Mike Powers
Cover photographs, front: *Black bear at Tenaya Lake (photo by Bjorn Bakstad);* back: *taking in the vista of Tuolumne Meadows*
Photo on page 208: *Yosemite National Park is a great place to create family memories.*
All photos by authors unless noted otherwise

Library of Congress Cataloging-in-Publication Data is on file for this title at https://lccn.loc.gov/2018044424.

Mountaineers Books titles may be purchased for corporate, educational, or other promotional sales, and our authors are available for a wide range of events. For information on special discounts or booking an author, contact our customer service at 800-553-4453 or mbooks@mountaineersbooks.org.

Printed on FSC®-certified materials

ISBN (paperback): 978-1-68051-152-9
ISBN (ebook): 978-1-68051-153-6

An independent nonprofit publisher since 1960

ADVENTURING WITH KIDS

CONTENTS

The spectacular vistas in Yosemite inspire rapturous delight even in little travelers.

INTRODUCTION

It's one of the big destinations, isn't it? The landscape of Yosemite National Park is largely responsible for the launching of the National Park Service (NPS) and the very idea of creating national parks. This place has been deeply meaningful to many people, including some, like Ansel Adams and John Muir, whose fame helped cement Yosemite as an essential part of our national heritage. When planning a vacation to such a venerated place, how do you decide what is most important for your family to see or do? We struggled to answer this question.

As seasoned national park explorers, we knew our kids weren't as inspired by big views as we are, but we wondered if *famous* sights might pique their interest. Were there hidden gems here that we would find only if we looked past the icons of the park? What could we do to create lasting memories that our children would carry into adulthood, inspiring them to embrace the protection of these kinds of places? In the end we decided to blend iconic sights, popular hikes, and some off-the-beaten-trail activities. By sharing our research, planning, and impressions of our time in Yosemite, we hope to help your family experience memorable and exciting adventures that will bring you closer to each other and to nature.

TOP FIVE TIPS FOR VACATIONING IN YOSEMITE WITH KIDS

Through many family vacations, during which our kids ranged in age from infants to teenagers, and which involved all sorts of camping, hiking, and adventuring, we have developed tips to help you have the best family vacation possible. Although some of this advice applies to any family trip, here are our top five tips for making the most of your Yosemite vacation.

1. Get out of the car.

Yosemite has some of the most widely recognized sights of any park. As you exit the tunnel off the South Entrance to the Yosemite Valley, the views will simply stop you in your tracks. The "big ones"—Yosemite Falls, El Capitan, and Half Dome—form a breathtaking panorama that defies belief. High up in the Tuolumne Meadows area, stunning lakes reflect the granite peaks surrounding them, arresting you with their beauty.

While adults can have a perfectly enjoyable trip sight-seeing from the car, kids generally cannot. Children are experimental and experiential by nature. They need to inter-act with the world around them using all of their senses. According to experts in psychology, when we experience events with more than one of our senses, our memories are deeper and more lasting. Just think of how you feel when a song from your past comes on the radio. "It takes me right back," we say. Or how about the scent of ozone after a thunder-and-lightning storm? If you've smelled that after feeling the vibrations of the thunderous concussions of sound, you will be transported back to that memory when-ever you smell it again. This is what we try to create for our children—memories that will last their lifetime and come flooding back with the smell of pine needles in the forest or the warmth of sun on their face.

To build memories that your family can share for years to come, and to create a sense of responsibility and stewardship toward places like Yosemite, nothing beats actually getting out on the trail. While exploring the outdoors, your kids will engage all of their senses. They will smell the damp and fecund forest as they run down the trail. They will see the foamy rush of whitewater as they cross a log bridge over a river and hear the squawk of a jay or the screech of a hawk when they stop for a snack along the way. These are the types of experiences you can create during a family trip to Yosemite that will leave indelible impressions.

All times of year are beautiful in Yosemite National Park. (Photo by Katie Grullón)

Having fun outside like these kids are is a great reason to get out of the car.

If that task seems daunting, read on. We are here to help you on that journey, and we promise it will be worth it for both you and your kids!

2. Download your digital content prior to departure.

Although Yosemite is located in the densely populated state of California, many parts of the park are far from civilization and thus wireless and cellular coverage are spotty or nonexistent. While some spots along the road have cell coverage, you cannot count on having service. Some of the lodges have Wi-Fi access and cell coverage, but it is often slow and sometimes can only be accessed by guests. If you expect to use the internet to plan your vacation once you arrive, you will be out of luck. Download all the digital resources you are using to plan your vacation ahead of time. Remember that this approach applies to digital content that you may want for your kids while the family is in the car. You won't be able to stream videos or music for the kiddos, so download what you think they will want before starting out. A good compromise on the device debate is to use audiobooks. You can download digital audiobooks from many places, including for free from most local libraries. This way your kids have something to listen to, but they can still look out the window. The hard part may be getting everyone to agree on a title.

Another great activity while in the car, or while sitting in camp, is the Junior Ranger program. This program is available at all the National Parks, and in Yosemite kids can join for a small fee. Your kids get an age-appropriate booklet with activities. Once they complete a certain number, they are awarded a Junior Ranger Badge during a swearing-in ceremony with a park ranger at a visitors center. The activities typically involve looking for certain sights or animals within the park, and they are educational and fun. Participating in this program encourages kids to become stewards of our national parks, which we believe is very important.

Earning a Junior Ranger badge gives kids a sense of accomplishment.

3. Have realistic expectations.

In 2016 more than five million people visited this popular park. These visitors tend to be concentrated in time and place. Weather limits the season when the high country is open and relatively snow free, and many of the must-see sights are concentrated in one spot: the Yosemite Valley. If you aren't prepared mentally, you may find yourself disappointed and frustrated.

On our first trip to the Valley in 2015, Abby had a sobbing breakdown after the family's first day of exploring. There were so many people, many of whom seemed to have little conservation and preservation ethic, traffic was horrendous, and access to hiking was limited. Our expectations simply didn't match the reality of visiting such a popular place. By sharing our knowledge in this book, we hope to help you avoid such disappointment. Adjusting your expectations and making a concerted effort to be patient will improve your chances of having a much better experience.

When visiting the sights in the Valley region of the park, be prepared for incredibly large numbers of people in a compact geographical area, many of whom come into the Valley on day trips each morning and leave each evening. Narrow, one-lane roads can make for quite a traffic jam during these hours. In addition to knowing what to expect, you can take a few steps to minimize the negative effect these conditions may have on your vacation.

First, we recommend you camp in the Valley if possible to eliminate time spent sitting in lines of traffic waiting to enter and exit it each day. Getting a camping spot in the Valley is difficult, but with a bit of strategy, you will find one well situated for the activities you and your family have planned. The Yosemite Camping and Lodging chapter contains information on securing a campsite or a room at a park lodge or hotel. If you are not fortunate enough to score accommodations in the Valley and must instead drive in each day, the following advice will help you mitigate the problems that come with the latter.

In the Yosemite Valley you are surrounded by great views, most of which are up.

While in the Valley, plan to use the free shuttle. If you are driving in each morning, park your car in the designated parking area near Yosemite Valley Lodge. If this lot is full, there are two other large visitor parking areas farther down the road. The main road through the Valley area is one-way, so you may have to drive the whole convoluted loop in order to park. The free shuttle stops at all the main hiking attractions and runs continuously throughout the day and evening. Pick up and study a shuttle map to make sure you wait on the correct side of the road. In the busiest months, the shuttle can fill up and will sometimes pass you by, leaving you to hope the next one has more room. You should expect to spend up to a third of your day waiting for and riding on the shuttle buses.

If that sounds miserable to you, may we suggest biking? Unlike many national parks where there is no trail riding and roads are

Allowing your kids to take small risks outdoors gives them confidence.

narrow and without shoulders, making biking unpleasant or dangerous, Yosemite Valley is ideal for family biking! A large, paved, mostly level bike and pedestrian path circles the Valley. This trail should be fine for children of all ages, as long as they can balance a bike. You will need to bring your own or rent them; learn more in Adding Adventure to Your Trip, later in the book. Pedaling two wheels gives you time to look at the amazing granite domes and cascading falls all around you. Much of the path follows the edge of meadows where you can often spot deer. Whether you are commuting into the Valley each day or staying at one of the accommodations there, we can think of no more enjoyable way to visit this part of the park.

If you are commuting into the Valley, consider coming and going at nonpeak times. Your family may want to get up really early and bring breakfast to eat in the car on the way in. To avoid the bulk of the traffic, plan to arrive before 8:00 a.m. Keep in mind that because the campgrounds outside the Valley area are quite far away, you will need to leave camp very early! Eating breakfast in the car can speed up the process, allowing everyone to sleep a little later. Just make sure to clean up any evidence of food from your car before leaving it for the day. Bears have been known to break into cars just to investigate an empty wrapper lying on the dashboard.

Also, think about bringing a picnic-style dinner with you each day. Then, when the rest of the crowd hits the road to head back to camp for dinner, you can grab a picnic spot along one of the meadows and enjoy the evening until the crowds thin and the roads are clearer. While this approach will get you back to camp later in the evening, we found that preferable to sitting in traffic with hungry, tired children. Plus, you'll get to enjoy the often spectacular sunsets in the Valley.

The final expectation that you may need to reset is about the wilderness awareness of many visitors. In parts of this park, we witnessed blatant disregard of and disrespect for nature and other people. We were so disappointed to see people feeding the animals, marching off-trail all over, wearing inappropriate clothing (down to almost no clothing at all), making noise, playing loud music, and being pushy. It is difficult to enjoy a family vacation with all that going on around you, but you cannot control other people. It is best to recognize that you may be faced with these behaviors and educate *your* family on stewardship of the park and respect for others.

If all this proves to be overwhelming for your family, we suggest you head up to the Glacier Point area. From there you can see the main attractions of the Valley without the crowds. It is quieter, cleaner, and less visited. Our family enjoyed hiking in the Valley first and then getting to view the places we hiked to from Glacier Point later. We do recommend that you visit the Valley and hike some of its trails, while trying to ignore the ill-behaved people around you. You can rest assured that your time in Glacier Point and up around Tuolumne Meadows will be much more peaceful.

4. Start easy and leave extra time.

As you begin selecting hikes, we caution you to start easy and leave yourself plenty of time. When visiting Yosemite with kids, make your first hike or outing less challenging than the second so that they don't get discouraged right off the bat. And allow extra time because, unlike adults, who are often focused on making it to the destination, kids are much more interested in enjoying the journey. Leave ample time for breaks, stopping to check out a creek or flower along the way, or anything else that little ones might find interesting. Kids need time to explore, and it is up to you to leave time in the schedule for them to discover new things. This book's hiking descriptions cover a wide range of hike times, because that calculation depends on so many factors: age, fitness level, number of breaks for snacks or picnics, and time allowed for exploration. Track your first few shorter outings to get a feel for how fast you hike as a family unit, and then use that knowledge to better estimate the longer hikes.

5. Bring plenty of the essentials.

If young people are not enjoying themselves outside, it is almost always due to one of two things—they are either hungry or uncomfortable (feeling chilled or overheated or suffering from sore feet). Bring plenty of water, trail mix, granola, nuts, fruit, and even candy bars. We've lost count of the number of times we've been out with our kids and they started whining and getting grouchy, only to take a five-minute snack break and be back in high spirits and raring to go. Napoleon Bonaparte once said that "an army marches on its stomach," and this is even more true of children.

Second, being outside means being exposed to the elements, which brings adventure but also risks—always be prepared. We carry an extra fleece jacket or sweatshirt with us, even on short hikes, and raingear on medium or longer jaunts. It is also wise to bring sunscreen: Yosemite's high elevation means

Warm kids are happy kids! (Photo by Katie Grullón)

higher-intensity UV rays and more chance of sunburn. In addition, the many beautiful lakes in the Tuolumne Meadows region are host to mosquitoes during the summer, so have your insect repellent handy. There are more detailed checklists later in the book, but food, water, and protection against the elements are always the most important items.

Crystal-clear water in Tuolumne Meadows

HOW TO USE THIS BOOK

We've selected family-friendly hikes and activities centered around children and what they like to see and do. These outings are both suitable for kids and enjoyable for parents and guardians. We focus on four regions of the park: Yosemite Valley, Glacier Point, the high country of Tuolumne Meadows and Tioga Road, and Wawona. Each regional chapter includes a detailed map featuring recommended hiking trails. In the descriptions, we give specifics for what we ourselves have researched. For many hikes, you can go farther or start elsewhere; park resources will help you discover more as you build your Yosemite adventures (see Resources). We'll help you plan a successful Yosemite trip with tips for vacationing, sample itineraries, best bets, and adventures beyond hiking—all with families in mind.

The following chapter, Planning Your Yosemite Family Vacation, provides helpful advice for navigating the park's website, where to find more information on lodging, considerations for what time of year to visit, as well as what methods of travel can get you there, with our thoughts on the advantages and disadvantages of each. The chapter highlights are the suggested itineraries for trips lasting three, five, or seven days, followed by a brief description of the types of activities we recommend for adding adventure to your family vacation.

Up next is the Best Bets chapter, which highlights our recommended activities for each region of the park. You may have very little background on Yosemite, or perhaps you have already identified a long list of attractions you want to see. Either way, this section will help you find those attractions and ensure that you won't miss out on any hidden gems you didn't know about. The chapter finishes with a review of some of the wildlife you may encounter.

In the heart of the book, the Yosemite Adventures by Region chapter, we review all the hikes and other activities that our family has vetted. We provide you with our insights on the aspects our kids enjoyed and disliked, what you can expect, what time of day to visit (if applicable), and plenty of pictures to whet your appetite. Each hiking route begins with an info block that lists crucial information: distance, elevation gain, estimated time, and directions to the trailhead. If you feel these basics about a given hike line up with your family's particular capabilities, read on for greater detail to confirm that it's a good match. Every family should find plenty of activities that suit them; we thoroughly researched all the family-friendly options to choose the ones most suitable for kids of all ages.

Next we share suggestions for backpacking, including an overview of the High Sierra Camps, followed by a chapter reviewing all of the park's camping and lodging options, as well as a few others nearby. Finally, we end by highlighting some of the key safety measures parents should consider as they plan their family's trip. A series of checklists helps make sure that you don't leave behind any important items. You'll find everything you need to begin to plan a memorable family vacation to Yosemite within these pages—get started!

Opposite: The scale of everything is large in Yosemite.

Sharing a child's wonder in nature makes an experience more fulfilling for adults. (Photo by Katie Grullón)

PLANNING YOUR YOSEMITE FAMILY VACATION

Planning any sort of trip comes down to a few basic questions: where and when you'll go, how you'll get there, where you'll stay, and what you'll do while you're there. The following sequence works for us when planning our family park trips.

First, go to the maps section on Yosemite National Park's official website (see Resources), where you can download and print a park map. Alternatively, ask the park staff to mail it to you, which they will usually do for free. It helps to have this big foldout map next to you as you plan. We write all over ours as we make decisions, and it becomes a major part of the trip planning.

If you plan to hike, we recommend picking up the free small trail maps available at any ranger station once you are in the park. These maps cover Tuolumne Meadows, Crane Flat and White Wolf, Glacier Point, Yosemite Valley, and Wawona, and they offer more detailed information on the main hiking routes, shuttle information, and parking. Be aware that they are *not* all to scale (particularly the Tuolumne Meadows area map). Failing to realize that may make for a much longer day than you anticipated.

By "liking" the park's Facebook page, you will have up-to-date information on closures, schedules, activities, and more. The official concessionaire of Yosemite, Aramark, has a helpful website, www.travelyosemite.com, and you can subscribe to their e-newsletter or follow them on Facebook or Twitter to keep up with special events they host. Now you are ready to start the hard-core planning!

Every recommended sight or adventure is listed according to the regions mentioned earlier: Yosemite Valley, Glacier Point,

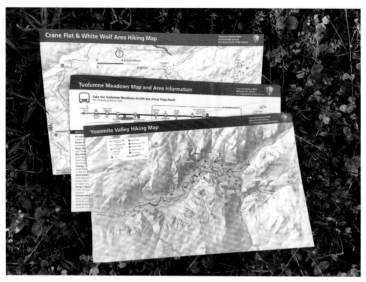

These smaller, easy-to-carry hiking maps are very handy reference tools.

Tuolumne Meadows (including areas along Tioga Road), and Wawona. Due to its lack of activities for families and far-north location, we exclude the Hetch Hetchy region (see sidebar). As you plan, keep track of the regions for each thing you want to do so you can figure out how to group them in order to minimize your time in the car.

Consider how much adventure you want to add to your trip. As we have mentioned, there are dozens of options for hiking, but you can also choose from horseback riding, backpacking, boating, bicycling, bus tours, and even rock climbing. We have provided all the information, organized into their respective regions, you need to learn about and book these adventures. Each region's activities are reviewed with kids in mind.

Decide what attractions in Yosemite you simply must see in order to feel like you got the most out of your visit. The Yosemite Adventures by Region and Best Bets chapters will help with this, but you should also talk to friends, search the internet, or

HETCH HETCHY

In 1913, stemming partly from the effects of the 1906 San Francisco earthquake and resulting fire, an act of Congress allowed the State of California to build a dam across the Hetch Hetchy Valley. While this reservoir supports 2.8 million people in the San Francisco area, its construction also destroyed the once beautiful valley that some people said rivaled Yosemite Valley. Despite the divided public opinion around this area's history, many people find this region away from the often-crowded, more popular areas of the park to be a breath of fresh air. Although Hetch Hetchy offers quiet and relative solitude, its remoteness is often a drawback when traveling with children. Before you decide whether to include it on your itinerary, keep the following factors in mind.

Hetch Hetchy is accessed via a winding, twisting two-hour drive from the Valley. Now that water fills the valley, there are precious few places to hike. The only kid-friendly hike in the area is the journey to Wapama Falls. The 5.5-mile hike with 200 feet of elevation gain leads to the towering 1400-foot falls—imagine how tall the falls were before the valley was flooded! The two other official trails (to Smith Peak and the Poopenaut Trail) are quite strenuous. Also, this region has no lodging for day hikers or services. A backpacker's campground and a ranger station here cater to the more serious backpackers who frequent the area.

call the park in the off-season to get other opinions. Often when our friends hear that we are planning a trip, they will say, "Oh, you must see X!" or "Don't miss Y!" As you follow the next steps, keep track of where, by region, the things on your to-do list are found. As you organize your favorites, you may find that you don't need to visit every region in order to feel you've hit all the high points.

Shared adventures strengthen family bonds.

Even as you're musing about your dream itinerary, be aware that there are time constraints on your Yosemite vacation. You can refer to our section on suggested itineraries (found later in this chapter) for stays of various lengths. Usually you can find an itinerary that is close to what you are planning and then customize it for your own situation.

Once you know what you want to do, organize your information based on the region your preferred activities are in, choose the regions you will visit and decide how much time you can spend in each, and finally make your lodging choices accordingly. Most regions of the park have both camping and indoor-lodging options, so you never have to stay too far from the action. However, many of the reservable options fill up as soon as they become available, up to twelve months in advance. Make sure to plan at least nine to twelve months ahead of time if you can. But if you find yourself making more last-minute plans, don't worry! There are a lot of first-come, first-served options out there too. Our Yosemite Camping and Lodging chapter will help you plan for any contingency.

Now all you have to do is figure out how you are going to get there. There are limitless variations on transportation depending on where you live, but it basically comes down to driving in your own vehicle, flying to a nearby airport and renting a car, taking a train, or some combination of these steps that might include renting a recreational vehicle (RV). Each of these options has implications for where you will stay as well.

The fun part is filling in your itinerary with the exciting adventures that we have listed by region. This book gives you all the information you need to create a journey that will engage and excite your children, building wonderful memories to last a lifetime. Planning the trip is a big part of the fun, so read on and start dreaming about your Yosemite vacation!

WHERE TO GO

Although Yosemite National Park encompasses more than 748,000 acres, the majority, about 94 percent, is designated wilderness. Even though that leaves only 6 percent that is easily accessible, the task of planning a trip here can be daunting. To help you get started, we tackle the park by region, highlighting each area's hikes, sights, and activities. Depending on the length of your trip, our suggestions can help you decide which region to focus on, or perhaps help you plan time to visit all of them.

Yosemite National Park is almost circular in shape, crossed from east to west by Tioga Road. Tuolumne Meadows is located at the eastern end of the road, while the other main areas are on the western end. The northern side of Tioga Road is mostly wilderness that can be difficult to access, although the Hetch Hetchy Reservoir is directly accessible by road. To the south the Wawona region boasts a grove of giant sequoias and some areas of historical interest.

Granite peaks and verdant meadows make up the Yosemite high country.

This book focuses on the areas of greatest interest to the most people: Yosemite Valley, Glacier Point, Tuolumne Meadows, and Wawona. We believe these regions hold the most accessible and interesting activities for your family and they are in the closest proximity to each other, making them appropriate for a single extended visit.

WHEN TO GO

While planning our first visit to Yosemite we were shocked at the variation in weather and temperatures between the popular Yosemite Valley and the less visited but still popular Tuolumne Meadows. Often, looking at a map will not give you the full picture. Unless you are used to looking at topographical maps, you can easily miss the changes in elevation on a road or trail map. While the Valley sits at around 4000 feet above sea level, Tuolumne Meadows rests at around

8600 feet above sea level—more than 4000 feet higher! The average temperatures of these two areas vary dramatically. In fact, Tioga Road is typically snowed in until sometime in May and occasionally until late June. The campgrounds in the high country open much later, and the snow can return as early as mid-September, making for a very short open season. Yosemite Valley is usually snow free by mid-April, with temperatures soaring into the upper eighties and low nineties from June through September. What do these statistics mean for your planning purposes? First,

Fall can be a beautiful time to visit, plus the crowds have usually thinned by then. (Photo by Katie Grullón)

if you would like to see both the Valley and Tuolumne Meadows, you will need to limit your window of time to midsummer through September or plan to make multiple trips, depending on where you want to camp. Keep that in mind as you examine your availability dates and plan your trip.

Second, you will need to pack accordingly. While you may experience some sweaty hiking days in the Valley, your kids may get quite cold in the evenings or when visiting the higher elevations. If you plan to visit multiple locations in one vacation, bringing clothes and bedding for both hot and cold weather is essential.

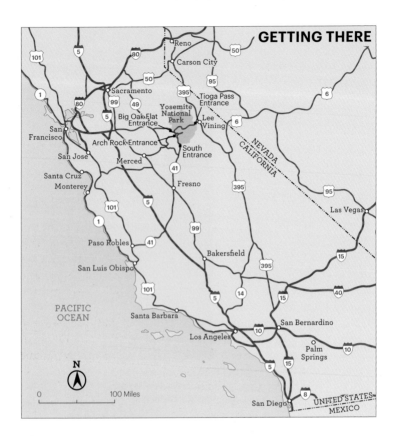

GETTING THERE

You have probably already thought about how you will travel to the park. The following notes offer some points you may not have considered.

By Car or RV

As you can see on the map above, Yosemite National Park has only a few main entry points. From the east you can enter the park only at the Tioga Pass Entrance, and Tioga Road is closed for most of the year. Before you plan to enter here, confirm that

Legend

—⑤— Interstate Highway	⌇ River	🅟 Picnic Area
—⑨⑨— US Highway	▭ Lake	⑴ Restrooms
—④①— State Highway	▬ Park	🅖 Gas Station
——— Other Road	▬ Shuttle Route	🅣 Trailhead
---------- Dirt Road	▪ Point of Interest	🅘 Information
-------- Featured Trail	Ⓐ Campground	🅡 Ranger Station
----------- Other Trail	Ⓐ High Sierra Camp	🅢 Shuttle Service
——— Bike Path	🅟 Parking	🄸 Shuttle Stop

the road is open, which is usually from June to October. This is the closest entrance to Tuolumne Meadows. Coming in via one of the western entrances will mean a two-to-three hour drive to reach Tuolumne Meadows on the winding, twisting Tioga Road.

From the south you enter the park at the South Entrance in the Wawona area. Although the distance to Yosemite Valley is relatively short as the crow flies, again the road twists and changes elevation so much that the drive from that entrance to the Valley can take one and a half to two hours.

The third option is to enter on the western side of the park. The Hetch Hetchy Entrance to the northwest provides access to the Hetch Hetchy Reservoir and the backcountry. Moving to the south of that entrance is the Big Oak Flat Entrance station, near the Hodgdon Meadow Campground. Once inside the park here, you can drive along Big Oak Flat Road to reach the Valley located below. Finally, the Arch Rock Entrance, the closest to the Yosemite Valley, is situated along El Portal Road.

Where you choose to enter will depend on where you decide to stay and which regions you plan to visit. Keep in mind that using roads outside the park will usually be faster, even if the route is longer, than using the roads inside the park. The main exception is if you need to get from one side to the other. In that case Tioga Road is your best bet when it's open.

Finally, if you plan on coming in an RV, keep in mind that there are a few restrictions on where you can travel, and parking spaces for large rigs are fairly limited. Glacier Point Road, Mariposa Road, and Hetch Hetchy Road all have restrictions that affect RVs of longer lengths and most trailers as well. Check the park website's Plan Your Visit section for the latest details on these restrictions, as they sometimes change. Also, if you don't have much experience driving an RV, make sure you are up for the challenge of driving these large vehicles on the park's steep and winding roads.

By Air

Yosemite National Park is almost due east of San Francisco, so any of the airports in the Bay Area make good destinations if you plan on flying in and renting a car to get to the park. San Jose (SJC) and Oakland (OAK) International airports are your best bets, as they are on the east side of the bay, so you won't have to fight as much traffic or cross a toll bridge. Sacramento (SMF) International airport is another good option that is actually about fifteen minutes closer to the park by car. However, Reno-Tahoe International Airport (RNO) would be our recommendation. Flights there are often cheaper than the alternatives and still leave you within a three-hour drive of Yosemite, provided you enter from the east side's Tioga Entrance station near Tuolumne Meadows—perhaps our favorite area.

Flying into Reno may also allow you to see stunning Lake Tahoe by detouring a few hours, a rewarding choice, particularly if you're visiting from far away. From there, the drive south to Yosemite runs along the edge of the Sierra Nevada, a far more scenic route than the crowded drive through California's Central Valley. In fact, this route passes through the town of Lee Vining, which lies right on the shores of Mono Lake—an amazing geologic wonder all its own.

National parks offer wonderful opportunities for kids to get hands-on with nature.

Other options to access the Tioga Entrance include Las Vegas International (LAS), but that is roughly a five-and-a-half hour drive. Los Angeles has a host of airports as well, but to reach Yosemite from LAX you will have to drive at least five hours—likely more due to LA's famous traffic congestion. We recommend finding an airport farther north.

By Train

Amtrak has north-south and east-west lines that will get riders as close as Reno, to the northeast, and Merced, west of the park. From these stops families can transfer to a bus or rent a car. If parents don't want to spend a lot of time driving and can pack relatively light, consider this approach.

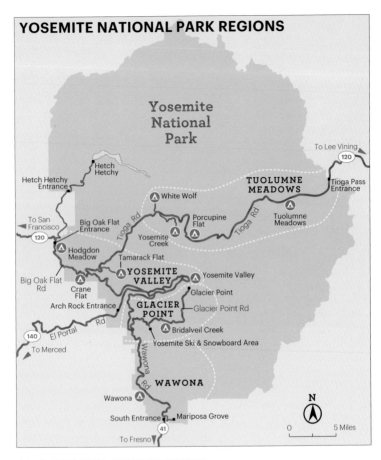

YOSEMITE NATIONAL PARK REGIONS

Yosemite National Park

To Lee Vining
120

Hetch Hetchy

Hetch Hetchy Entrance

TUOLUMNE MEADOWS

Tioga Pass Entrance

White Wolf

To San Francisco
120

Big Oak Flat Entrance

Porcupine Flat

Tuolumne Meadows

Yosemite Creek

Tioga Rd

Hodgdon Meadow

Tamarack Flat

Big Oak Flat Rd

YOSEMITE VALLEY

Yosemite Valley

Crane Flat

Glacier Point

Arch Rock Entrance

GLACIER POINT

Glacier Point Rd

140
El Portal Rd

To Merced

Bridalveil Creek

Yosemite Ski & Snowboard Area

Wawona Rd

WAWONA

Wawona

South Entrance

Mariposa Grove

41

To Fresno

N

0   5 Miles

SUGGESTED ITINERARIES

Planning a trip to a national park can be challenging. For example, without having been there before, how can you get a true sense of how long it will take to visit various locations? Is it possible to drive from one side of the park to the other in a single day? Where should you stay, and how should you organize your hikes and adventures? To give you an idea of how you might plan your time in Yosemite, we have provided sample itineraries for various trip lengths ranging from one to seven days.

Because there are several entrance points to the park, rather than organizing the itineraries day by day, we simply state how much time you should spend in each region. That way you can arrange the days in a way that suits you and your family. Please use the itineraries as guides you can customize to fit your situation and the activities you are most looking forward to. The suggested itineraries below list "must-see-and-do" attractions as well as lodging options. For more detail on each of these attractions, consult the Yosemite Adventures by Region chapter. For overnight options, see Resources. These itineraries exclude travel time to Yosemite from your home or whichever airport you fly into.

Three-Day Itineraries

Due to the considerable distance between Tuolumne Meadows and Yosemite Valley, it is difficult for families to fully explore both regions in three days. To really experience Yosemite Valley and Tuolumne Meadows, you'll need to spend two days in each place and one day in Glacier Point. Mix and match these options or choose to focus two days on either the Valley or Tuolumne, and then spend one day in the other and skip Glacier Point. You won't take it *all* in, but this is still a good compromise.

Yosemite Valley: 2 Days

If you prefer a Yosemite Valley and Glacier Point itinerary, we suggest exploring the Valley first. From Glacier Point overlooks you will then be able to look across the Valley and see many of the locations you may have hiked to. Kids love being able to get a feel for the grand scale of the trails they hiked the previous day. They will enjoy the scenic value of Glacier Point so much more after they have a personal connection to all the sights they can take in.

Granite and waterfalls define the Yosemite Valley.

Must-See-and-Do Attractions

These options may vary somewhat based on the ages of your children. For older children and teens, the Mist Trail tops the list, and for families with younger children, a morning devoted to Happy Isles is time well spent. See below for further recommendations, but be sure to check our detailed trip reports to assess whether they are appropriate for your children. Note that we suggest more activities than can possibly fit into two days, knowing that no family will choose all of the suggestions.

- Mist Trail: Half day
- Happy Isles: Half day
- Bike or raft the Valley floor (Sentinel and Cook Meadow Trail or the Merced River): Half day
- Mirror Lake: Half day

Camping and Lodging Options

The best option is to stay in the Yosemite Valley itself. If there are no campsites, canvas tents, or rooms available inside the Valley, consider outside campgrounds within an hour's drive, which will increase your time in the car but still allow you daily access to the Valley.

- Yosemite Valley campgrounds: Camp 4, North Pines Campground, Lower Pines Campground, Upper Pines Campground
- Yosemite Valley lodging: The Majestic Yosemite Hotel (formerly The Ahwahnee Hotel), Yosemite Valley Lodge (formerly Yosemite Lodge), Half Dome Village (formerly Curry Village), Housekeeping Camp
- Camping near Yosemite Valley: Bridalveil Creek Campground in Glacier Point, about forty-five minutes south of the Valley; Hodgdon Meadow, Crane Flat Camp, and Tamarack Flat Campgrounds, about forty-five minutes north of the Valley

Glacier Point: 1 Day

This area is serviced by a long and twisting road that takes you to a high ridge overlooking the Yosemite Valley, providing a new perspective on its amazing features.

Must-See-and-Do Attractions

- Taft Point: Half day
- Washburn Point: 30 minutes
- Glacier Point: 60 minutes
- Four-Mile Trail: 4–6 hours, recommended for teens and adults

Campgrounds in Glacier Point Area

Bridalveil Creek Campground is the only option in this region, but if you already have a camping spot in the Valley, we recommend you keep it in order to prevent moving camp more than necessary. See options above.

Tuolumne Meadows and Tioga Road: 2 Days

To the north and east of the world-famous Yosemite Valley is Tuolumne Meadows. More remote and secluded than other parts of

Time on the beach will rank highly with your kids.

the park, this area was a favorite of esteemed visitors such as John Muir, Robert Underwood Johnson, and Edward Parsons, the Sierra Club's first director. Here you will find high mountain lakes, shallow and crystal clear; granite domes, seemingly unaffected by the ages; and a little bit of breathing space to appreciate the thin but fresh cool air. In this region, we also include some hikes at different points along Tioga Road.

Must-See-and-Do Attractions
o Hang out at and swim or hike along the south side of Tenaya Lake: 2–4 hours or more
o Climb Lembert or Pothole Dome: 2–4 hours
o Lyell Canyon: 2–4 hours or longer
o Tuolumne Meadows to Soda Springs and Parsons Lodge: 1–2 hours
o Gaylor Lakes: 2–4 hours

Along Tioga Road: 1 Day

Must-See-and-Do Attractions

- ○ Lukens Lake: 2–3 hours
- ○ May Lake: 2–3 hours
- ○ Tuolumne Grove of Giant Sequoias: 2 hours

Camping and Lodging Options

Although you won't find any grand lodging options in the region, two lodges offer comfortable canvas wall tents, and there are a lot of campgrounds spread along Tioga Road. There are also what are known as High Sierra Camps (HSC), which require some hiking to reach. We won't detail all these options here, but if you are interested in them, you can learn more in the Yosemite Campgrounds and Lodging chapter later in the book.

Finally, we also recommend a few campgrounds outside the Tioga Pass Entrance that are on Forest Service land. Normally we try to limit our reviews to facilities within the parks, but due to the difficulty of ensuring yourself a spot in the NPS campgrounds in this popular park, we chose to expand our limits a bit to help you secure a camping spot for your family!

- ○ Campgrounds along Tioga Road (from the east in Tuolumne Meadows, heading west): Tuolumne Meadows Campground, Porcupine Flat Campground, Yosemite Creek Campground, White Wolf Campground, Tamarack Flat Campground
- ○ Campgrounds on Forest Service land to the east of the Tioga Pass Entrance station: Tioga Lake Campground, Junction Campground, Ellery Lake Campground, Saddlebag Lake Campground, Big Bend Campground
- ○ Lodging options: Tuolumne Meadows Lodge, White Wolf Lodge

Five-Day Itinerary

If you plan to take an entire week off from work for your vacation, your family can experience Yosemite at a much more relaxed pace, limiting the stress that can come from trying to "do it all" in a short amount of time and in a crowded place. Five days will also allow you to

Frothy cascades where water meets granite

see and experience things in both the Valley and Tuolumne Meadows regions.

Assuming you will travel on bookend weekends and have five full days in the park, here are our suggested activities. Remember, switch the days around in a way that makes sense based on where you enter and depart the park.

Yosemite Valley: 2 Days

Must-See-and-Do Attractions

This selection may vary based on the ages of your children. For older children and teens, Mist Trail tops the list, and for families with younger children, a morning devoted to Happy Isles is time well spent. See below for further recommendations, but be sure to check our detailed trip reports to assess whether they are appropriate for your children. Note that we suggest more activities than can possibly fit into two days—choose the suggestions best suited for your family.

- Mist Trail: Half day
- Happy Isles: Half day
- Bike or raft the Valley floor (Sentinel and Cook Meadow Trail or the Merced River): Half day
- Mirror Lake: Half day

Camping and Lodging Options

The best option for you is to stay in the Yosemite Valley itself. If you do not have a site or room there, some campgrounds outside the Valley will increase your time in the car but still allow you daily access to the Valley.

- Yosemite Valley campgrounds: Camp 4, North Pines Campground, Lower Pines Campground, Upper Pines Campground
- Yosemite Valley lodging: The Majestic Yosemite Hotel (formerly The Ahwahnee Hotel), Yosemite Valley Lodge (formerly Yosemite Lodge), Half Dome Village (formerly Curry Village), Housekeeping Camp
- Camping near Yosemite Valley: Bridalveil Creek Campground in Glacier Point, about forty-five minutes south of the Valley; Hodgdon Meadow, Crane Flat, and Tamarack Flat Campgrounds, about forty-five minutes north of the Valley

Glacier Point: 1 Day

This area is serviced by a long and twisting road that takes you to a high ridge overlooking the Yosemite Valley, providing a new perspective on the amazing features there.

Must-See-and-Do Attractions
- Taft Point: Half day
- Washburn Point: 30 minutes
- Glacier Point: 60 minutes
- Teens and adults can hike the Four-Mile Trail from here down to the Valley: 4–6 hours

Campground in Glacier Point area: Bridalveil Creek Campground is the only option in this region, but if you already have a camping spot in the Valley, we recommend you keep it in order to prevent moving camp more than is necessary.

Tuolumne Meadows and Tioga Road: 2 Days

This more remote region of the park offers high mountain lakes and granite domes.

Must-See-and-Do Attractions
- Hang out at and swim or hike along the south side of Tenaya Lake: 2–4 hours or more
- Climb Lembert or Pothole Dome: 2–4 hours
- Lyell Canyon: 2–4 hours or longer
- Tuolumne Meadows to Soda Springs and Parsons Lodge: 1–2 hours
- Gaylor Lakes: 2–4 hours

Along Tioga Road: 1 Day

If you have time, plan to stop at a few places as you drive Tioga Road.

Must-See-and-Do Attractions
- Lukens Lake: 2–3 hours
- May Lake: 2–3 hours
- Tuolumne Grove of Giant Sequoias: 2 hours

View from Parsons Lodge in Tuolumne Meadows

Camping and Lodging Options

- o Campgrounds along Tioga Road (from the east in Tuolumne Meadows, heading west): Tuolumne Meadows Campground, Porcupine Flat Campground, Yosemite Creek Campground, White Wolf Campground, Tamarack Flat Campground
- o Campgrounds on Forest Service land to the east of the Tioga Pass Entrance station: Tioga Lake Campground, Junction Campground, Ellery Lake Campground, Saddlebag Lake Campground, Big Bend Campground
- o Lodging options: Tuolumne Meadows Lodge, White Wolf Lodge

Seven Days and Beyond

If fortune has smiled upon you and graced you with seven days to spend in the park, rejoice! This leisurely timeframe will allow you to really enjoy yourselves. In addition to the suggestions in the three- and five-day itineraries, you could add in a backpacking trip to a High Sierra Camp, spend more time relaxing along the shores of Tenaya Lake, or even visit the southern part of the park to learn more about its history and see the largest of the Yosemite sequoias.

You might decide to stay in one of the regions a day longer to work your hikes around the schedule of the ranger-led hikes or to experience some of the Wawona area by horseback. You can also extend your regional stays by adding in or extending any of the other hikes we review in the shorter itineraries or choosing another hike or activity to keep your family engaged.

ADDING ADVENTURE TO YOUR TRIP

Yosemite offers plenty of adventures for families. From pedaling around the Valley to playing in the lakes and rivers to hiking, everyone will find an enjoyable activity. Kids who are comfortable with it may even enjoy getting above the crowds on a rope on one of the granite walls that line the Valley.

Hiking

The easiest, cheapest way to explore any national park is also the most engaging and best-paced way for kids to explore the outdoors. Walking along the trails allows for stops to look at bugs, examine beautiful rock formations, throw stick boats in the water, and absorb the scent of pine sap in the warm sun. With more than eight hundred miles of hiking trails, you are sure to find some trails that are just right for your family. The majority of this book is devoted to helping you find the trails that will get your family out for an enjoyable day of hiking.

Bicycling

While narrow roads with narrow to nonexistent shoulders make many national parks unsuitable for biking with kids, Yosemite Valley is the ideal location for biking adventures. With nearly flat terrain and wide bike paths along the entire length of the region, families can enjoy time spent bicycling together. Also remember that the more of your kids' senses you can stimulate,

From massive cascades to gentle streams, Yosemite has it all.

Even a brisk lake is welcome on a hot day.

the more likely they are to build lasting memories. Imagine cruising along, the breeze in your face, the sun on your back, and the swish of meadow grasses along the side of the trail. These bike trails allow you to avoid boring your kids by making them sit in the car as you wait for parking spots; instead you can engage their minds and bodies while traveling around the Valley.

Good news! You can bring your own bikes or rent some from two Valley locations: Yosemite Valley Lodge or Half Dome Village. The rental shops provide helmets and even offer ride-along attachments for kids who aren't pedaling on their own yet. The rentals are first-come, first-served, so get to the bike shop early on the morning you want to ride.

Horseback Riding

Yosemite National Park allows you to bring your own stock and provides a few corral areas for your use. Big Trees Stables is the only location that offers guided rides on a park horse. Located in the southwest part of the park in the Wawona area, close to the Pioneer Yosemite History Center, the stables are found in the main service area surrounding the Big Trees Lodge. You can choose to take a two-hour ride on a historical pioneer trail on muleback or horseback. Riders must be seven years old and at least forty-four inches tall. For more details on requirements, rates, and reservations, visit www.travelyosemite.com.

Watersports

If you've been a parent for long, you know that kids love water! There seems to be a magnetic pull between children of all ages and water, and Yosemite is a great park to play in the water with your kids. All of the park's water is open to swimming except for Hetch Hetchy and May Lake in the Tuolumne Meadows area, as they are used for drinking water. The rivers here are crystal clear and cold. Kids will marvel at how the water flows over the many-hued stones along the bottom, or they will enjoy tossing stones and watching them sink. The very clear lakes offer refreshing spots to stop and recharge.

Beyond swimming, you are welcome to bring your own personal, nonmotorized watercraft to the lakes and rivers and enjoy time paddling. Make sure you plan some time in your schedule to enjoy the watery side of Yosemite.

Boating

Yosemite offers opportunities to boat on both lakes and rivers. For younger children and families without much boating experience, we recommend starting with lakes. Lake water doesn't move much, if at all, which makes for a safer, less intimidating experience. Lake Tenaya in the Tuolumne Meadows area is a beautiful lake to float with very easy access points all along its northern side and at both ends.

Some sections of the rivers move slowly enough for kids to tube in, like parts of the Merced River through Yosemite Valley. There are designated launch areas along the Merced, and access points may be restricted when the water levels are high. Your best bet is to check in with a ranger the day you want to float to make sure you know which locations are safe for your family based on their abilities.

Keep in mind that all children must wear a personal flotation device (PFD) at all times when boating, and all boaters must wear one at certain times, such as during the high water season in the early spring. Our family does a lot of rafting, and we all—adults and children—always wear them when on the water, even if local land managers and agencies don't require them. We recommend you take such safety precautions for your family. You can find out more about boating locations and regulations on the park's website (see Resources).

Swimming

Do yourself a favor and make time for some water play. There are many safe places to let your kids get wet. Spots like Mirror Lake in the Valley and Tenaya Lake in the Tuolumne Meadows area are wonderful places to enjoy a hot afternoon. Bear in mind that there are also plenty of dangerous water locations. Many rivers are full, raging torrents in the spring, and the cold snow runoff has swept many visitors to their deaths, especially near the park's waterfalls. A ranger can direct you toward preferable locations and let you know if the water levels are safe on a given day.

Rock climbers setting up for the day near Tenaya Lake

Rock Climbing

Yosemite is a rock-climbing mecca. The soaring granite domes make for great climbing, and the hardness of the rock means climbers leave little in the way of a footprint. Almost every day of the summer you will be able to see climbers scaling the rock walls beside the roads. Although climbs up Half Dome and El Capitan tend to garner the most attention (for example, the

2017 rope-free ascent by Alex Honnold), there are other much more accessible and fun routes closer to the road. Driving Tioga Road west past Tenaya Lake, you will likely spot climbers throughout the day.

Unlike most parks, Yosemite offers climbing classes through the Yosemite Mountaineering School (YMS) and Guide Service. Beginners can take classes, and experienced climbers can participate in guided trips and rent gear. YMS guides are all either Wilderness First Responder–certified or hold a Wilderness Emergency Medical Technician (EMT) card. This service offers a fantastic chance to give your kids a bit of a thrill in a safe, educational environment, particularly older kids who like to get a bit of an adrenaline rush. Classes are usually seven hours long, so plan accordingly. For more information and to make reservations, visit www.travelyosemite.com.

Fishing

Yosemite offers many wonderful fishing opportunities. All the park's lakes are open to fishing year round, and its rivers are open from April through November. Visitors must follow all the usual fishing regulations for California, including having a fishing license that can be purchased online through the California Department of Fish and Wildlife (see Resources) or in the park at the Mountain Shop in Half Dome Village. Kids sixteen years of age and younger do not need a license.

Bus and Tram Tours

For a fee, Aramark offers guided bus and tram tours in the Valley and Glacier Point areas. These tours are low on the adventure scale, and while the guides share a lot of historical information about the sights, tours of this type usually bore most kids. Since the tours don't really engage the senses and can be quite long, kids may feel like they are sitting in school. Plus, the drivers of the free shuttle buses run by the National Park Service are often willing to provide much of the same information. If they don't readily volunteer, ask if they will share what they know.

BEST BETS

If you take the time and effort to journey across the country or even just the state of California to Yosemite National Park, you owe it to yourself to see a few things in order to get the most out of your experience. We sorted our "best bets" by region to make it easy for you to plan. Read through these suggestions, craft your own top activities list, and then read the detailed descriptions in the activities section to make sure they are truly a good fit for your family or group.

If your children are a bit older, consider a strenuous, yet memorable hike like Clouds Rest.

The Happy Isles Nature Center is hands-on, educational, and interesting for all ages.

YOSEMITE VALLEY

Ah, the famous Yosemite Valley. Growing up as a rock climber in Boulder, Colorado, Abby often dreamed of seeing the sights and climbing the heights of Yosemite Valley. Half Dome and El Capitan pepper the dreams of rock climbers everywhere. Yet even many people who don't rock climb know about the famous sights lining this granite valley. Thanks to artists like Ansel Adams many people have seen images of the icons of Yosemite. Now you get to see them in person. As our sixteen-year-old said, "Pictures can't show you how it really is. You have to come stand here and see it."

It is difficult to whittle these famous spots down to a list of the best. Some of what you choose to visit will depend on your family's abilities. Remember, you are in a valley, which means almost all the hiking goes *up*! How many hikes and the level of strenuousness you can tackle will depend on your kids—and your physical fitness.

First of all, if you can arrange it, enter the Valley the first time from the south along Wawona Road. Coming from this direction, you'll pass through the tunnel and emerge in the sun with views down the Valley! Beyond the tunnel, you can stop at a pullout to take in all the sights at once.

Once you are in the Valley, we highly recommend you pedal around the meadows that fill the Valley floor on a self-guided tour (see the Cycling the Valley map in the next chapter for a suggested route). Your family will enjoy it at any time in your trip—don't feel as if you must schedule it first. Although the entire loop spans 13 miles and the half loop spans 6.5 miles, biking along even a short section of the trail is pleasant. Your family may want to stop and swim in the Merced River (at the beach near Housekeeping Camp, for example), and you have a good chance of seeing deer and perhaps other creatures, especially in the morning and evening.

Although you can see it from many spots in the Valley, the short, level hike to Yosemite Falls is well worth the time for adults and kids of all ages to see this astounding sight

Happy Isles makes the best bets list for the younger set. The wandering path to it crosses the Merced River a few times and feels like a meander through an enchanted forest. Places where the river is wide and cool make great stopping and snacking locations. Kids will find a lot of interesting exhibits at the nature center (when it is open), but visiting it is optional.

Older kids (tweens and teens) who are in decent shape will not want to miss the Mist Trail as it climbs to the top of Vernal Fall. While this trail is mostly uphill on the way to the falls, hiking through the spraying mist toward the top generates a lot of excitement.

GLACIER POINT

People come to Glacier Point for the views. Since Glacier Point Road climbs up and out of the Yosemite Valley to the top of the plateau that forms one of its sides, the vistas are remarkable. While you may relish taking in the famous sights of the Valley from a lofty vantage, remember that children are not generally enchanted by views. They will likely be antsy from the car ride to the area and hoping to get out and see some action. While most guidebooks will steer you toward these fabulous overlooks, we have a few other suggestions and some ideas on how to help your kids enjoy the sights better. You can have a great family experience here too!

The first hike along the Glacier Point Road that we love for families is Taft Point. It offers something for people of all ages. There is a great creek crossing early on in the hike, so leave time for some leaf-boat races. Excellent rock formations along the trail invite scrambling and exploring. Eventually you come to "the fissures" and Taft Point itself. A unique geologic feature composed of cracks in the cliff walls you are hiking along, some fissures are only ten feet across, but others are much wider. While small children will require attentive adult supervision here, older kids and teens will love the thrill of the drop-off view of the Valley. (Learn more about this natural wonder in the Yosemite Adventures by Region chapter.)

Our other suggestion for hiking in the area is perfect for when your family needs to beat the crowds and find some peace and quiet. While few hikes in this area are advertised to the general public, a handful of trails here lead to backcountry campsites. These trails are open to anyone; you need a permit only if you are camping along them. If you are just day hiking, you will find solitude and a connection to nature unsurpassed elsewhere in Yosemite, because typically only the overnight backpackers use these trails.

One example is the hike to Westfall Meadow. Park near the sign to McGurk Meadow, and look for a faint trailhead across the street from that hike. On a gorgeous day in the busiest time of year, we saw no other people on this hike. Although it didn't have many exciting features for kids that we often look for, we all just enjoyed the quiet and the slower pace. We found some water to poke around in along a marshy point in the trail and even some snow for a short and sweet snowball fight!

Of the two main overlook points, Glacier Point and Washburn Point, we liked Washburn Point best. It was less crowded

The Tuolumne Meadows region contains many high mountain lakes.

and had excellent views of the east end of the Valley. We recommend you come here after hiking around the Valley, because your kids will really enjoy identifying places they have already been. Our boys were astonished to look out from Washburn Point, across the deep valley, to Vernal and Nevada Falls, which they had climbed to the previous day. Having a personal connection to the sights you see makes a huge difference.

TUOLUMNE MEADOWS

This high alpine region has a lot to offer families. Our favorite spot for relaxing in the area was on the west end of Lake Tenaya, where there is a big sandy beach area with beautiful views. There are other spots along the lake with beaches, including the picnic area off the main road and more secluded areas along the east end, just across the inlet river. Because the lake is shallow, the water is warmer than you might expect.

Expansive vistas along Gaylor Lakes Trail

We also loved climbing to the tops of some of the granite domes because of the panoramic views they offer. Lembert Dome is a wonderful choice for families who can hike a ways, and with a bit of extra effort you can extend your hike a reasonable distance to enjoy a picnic lunch on the shores of Dog Lake. Don't let the name fool you—this lake is gorgeous, but be sure to bring some mosquito repellent. Pothole Dome is great even for families with very young kids. Scrambling to the top of either one of these domes gives you an amazing view and sense of accomplishment, plus kids love the climbing and rock-scrambling aspects.

If you are looking to sample some of the alpine environment, two great hikes end at gorgeous lakes. The short but steep

Gaylor Lakes hike has commanding vistas at almost every point along the trail, whereas the Elizabeth Lake hike is longer but very moderate in elevation gain. The chain of lakes and streams in this area that reflect the surrounding granite peaks makes for a sublime setting.

Finally, the short hike across Tuolumne Meadows to Parsons Lodge and Soda Springs gives you a good taste of a bit of the history of the area. Here, John Muir and Robert Underwood Johnson first conceived of a national park to protect this area, and in 1889 John Lembert built the log structure protecting the natural soda spring. In addition to traversing the meadows, the more adventurous will get to taste pure soda water as it bubbles forth from the ground!

WAWONA

This region of the park has a different feel than the other areas, but it still has plenty to offer. The history of this area involves quite a bit more "civilization" and human presence than the more northern reaches of the park. You will see more buildings, green lawns, and historical markers here than in the other regions. As to its offerings, first, this is the location of the impressive Mariposa Grove of Giant Sequoias. For a sense of the park's history and what life in the West was like more than one hundred years ago, you can check out the Pioneer Yosemite History Center with its blacksmith shop and stagecoach rides. The Meadow Loop hiking trail here is flat and easy, and the trail up Chilnualna Fall can be tailored to the age range and fitness of your group. Finally, if you are looking for a guided horseback trip for your family, this is the only place in the park that offers it.

WILDLIFE

Yosemite is known primarily for its amazing granite formations and spectacular waterfalls, but it also has some interesting wildlife viewing opportunities for those who are interested.

Birds

Western scrub jay

Due to its wide range of elevations and habitats, some 250 species of birds make their homes in the park for at least part of the year. While the extensive birding opportunities are outside the scope of this book, the park's website and other literature from the visitor centers can help you identify the more commonly seen varieties such as Steller's jay, American robin, acorn woodpecker, common raven, and mountain chickadee.

Bears

Yosemite is also quite well known for its black bears, perhaps due to the strict measures taken throughout the park to prevent them from becoming habituated to human garbage and handouts as was prevalent in years past. Nowadays, the park has bear-resistant food lockers and trash cans in campsites and at trailheads, among other safety features, to help keep both the bears and humans safe.

There are between three hundred and five hundred bears within the park itself, and despite their name, the bears in this region tend to range in color from brown to blond rather than the jet-black more typical of other parts of North America. The prevalence of bears in the park can be intimidating for families visiting with children, and while precaution is warranted, no one has ever been killed or seriously injured by a black bear in Yosemite. If you are respectful of these animals and follow park regulations, the risk to you and your family is basically negligible.

When mule deer antlers are growing, they are covered in a fuzzy sheath called velvet.

Deer

Interestingly Yosemite is found at the intersection of the ranges of two species of deer, the large mammal that park visitors are most likely to encounter. The blacktail deer, which lives west of the Sierra Nevada, has a fairly broad tail that is black on the top and white on the underside. To the east of these mountains and in the park's higher regions is the slightly larger mule deer, so named because of its large ears. The mule deer also has black on its tail, but its tail is long and narrow—more like a thick rope. The hair of its rump and its tail is white, but the very tip of its tail is black. There is some debate as to the official classification of the deer in various regions of the park. However, most scientific resources consider the majority of the deer in the park to be the mule deer species, and indeed the ones we saw had a narrower, black-tipped tail.

It shouldn't be too hard for you and your family to get a view of these sleek creatures. Small groups of deer feed in many of

Can you spot the coyote?

the meadows in the Yosemite Valley and in Tuolumne Meadows early in the morning, in late afternoon, or at twilight. It is not uncommon to see them at these same times near various campgrounds that offer some amount of forage.

Other Wildlife

Yosemite is host to a wide variety of other animals that are much more furtive than the ones described above. The abundance of deer in the area provides an adequate prey base for a healthy population of mountain lions, but sightings of these elusive creatures are very rare. This big cat's smaller cousin is the bobcat, which preys primarily on small mammals such as mice and birds. It is still a long shot to ever see one of these furry critters, so count yourself lucky if you catch a glimpse of one.

The last predator to consider is the coyote, which is very clever and opportunistic when it comes to scavenging food.

Since they are less shy than their feline counterparts, it is fairly common to see them if you are in the park for an extended period and are willing to get off the beaten path. Although they might look larger due to their long legs and furry coats, which vary with the seasons, they are actually quite small, with an average weight of around twenty to thirty-five pounds, similar to a small to medium-sized dog.

Finally, one endangered species makes Yosemite its home. There are only a few hundred Sierra bighorn sheep left throughout the Sierra Nevada. A small number of these (fewer than seventy-five) live in the less frequented northwest corner of Yosemite, but park visitors sometimes spot them from the Tioga Road to the east of Tuolumne Meadows.

FINAL THOUGHTS ON SIGHTSEEING

While the recommendations above are our best bets by region, we encourage you to keep reading. Yosemite offers so much to see and do, and each family's adventure will be different. Read on for more ideas on specific hikes and experiences that your family will love.

Yosemite Valley is full of striking sights like this one of Bridalveil Falls.

YOSEMITE ADVENTURES BY REGION

The layout of Yosemite National Park presents an interesting organizational challenge for families as they plan their trip. It can be difficult to grasp the scale of this vast park! For our first trip, we grabbed a campsite in Hodgdon Meadows Campground near the Big Oak Flat Entrance, thinking it would be a quick drive to the Valley each morning and then later over to Tuolumne Meadows. How wrong we were! Not only is it quite a few miles to the Valley, it is also up a steep, winding road. Plus, the maps don't account for traffic. In this guide, we have done our best to divide the park into helpful regions, but keep in mind that driving the park's roads takes more time than you would expect.

THE VALLEY

Home to the park's most famous sights, Yosemite Valley is also the hub of the majority of activity. You will both soak up amazing sights and encounter hordes of people, but if you are prepared, you can also experience great joy.

For more than a century, people have stood in awe at the opening of Yosemite Valley as they tried to take in the grand sights: El Capitan, Yosemite Falls, Bridalveil Fall, Half Dome, and more. John Muir put it this way:

> *The far-famed valley came suddenly into view throughout almost its whole extent: the noble walls, sculptured into endless variety of domes and gables, spires and battlements and plain mural precipices, all a-tremble with the thunder tones of the falling water. The level bottom seemed to be dressed like a garden, sunny meadows here*

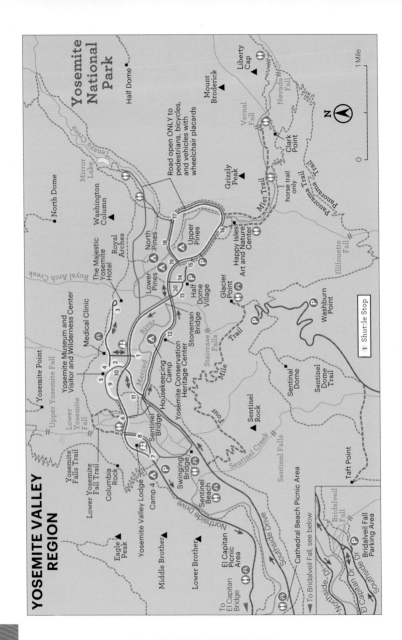

YOSEMITE VALLEY REGION

Yosemite National Park

N

0   1 Mile

Eagle Peak

Middle Brother

Lower Brother

To El Capitan Bridge

El Capitan Picnic Area

Columbia Rock

Yosemite Falls Trail

Lower Yosemite Fall Trail

Upper Yosemite Fall

Yosemite Point

Yosemite Fall

Lower Yosemite Fall

Camp 4

Yosemite Valley Lodge

Swinging Bridge

Sentinel Beach

Sentinel Bridge

Medical Clinic

Yosemite Museum and Visitor and Wilderness Center

Royal Arch Creek

The Majestic Yosemite Hotel

Royal Arches

Washington Column

North Dome

Mirror Lake

Half Dome

Tenaya Creek

Lower Pines

North Pines

Upper Pines

Stoneman Bridge

Half Dome Village

Happy Isles Art and Nature Center

Housekeeping Camp

Yosemite Conservation Heritage Center

Merced River

Staircase Falls

Four Mile Trail

Sentinel Rock

Sentinel Falls

Sentinel Creek

Sentinel Dome

Sentinel Dome Trail

Cathedral Beach Picnic Area

Northside Drive

Southside Drive

To Bridalveil Fall, see below

Glacier Point

Washburn Point

Grizzly Peak

Mist Trail

horse trail only

Panorama Trail

Illilouette Trail

Illilouette Fall

Vernal Fall

Clark Point

Nevada Fall

Mount Broderick

Liberty Cap

Road open ONLY to pedestrians, bicycles, and vehicles with wheelchair placards

Taft Point

Bridalveil Fall

Bridalveil Fall Parking Area

El Capitan Dr.

Southside Dr.

Northside Dr.

1 Shuttle Stop

*and there and groves of pine and oak, the river of Mercy
sweeping in majesty through the midst of them and flash-
ing back the sunbeams.*

As poetic as that description may be, the majesty of the Valley
can never be captured with words—you have to see it for yourself to appreciate its grandeur.

Things You Need to Know

As we mentioned, you must expect huge numbers of people in
the Valley. This is not the place to seek solitude. Even hikes of
over 1 mile, usually enough to discourage less committed hikers, are often crowded with a lot of people. It can be difficult
to appreciate nature under these conditions, but if you want
to see the Valley, you will have to brave the masses. Riding
the free shuttle and having realistic expectations about how
long it will take to get places will help, and using bicycles to
access trailheads once you are settled in the Valley is even better. Remember that you are in a place full of important history
and iconic sights, so relax and enjoy the ride no matter how
congested the path.

Hiking Adventures

Choose from the Valley's iconic destinations, including Vernal
Fall, Bridalveil Fall, and Lower Yosemite Fall.

 Mirror Lake

The easy, rolling hike to this wide, still spot in the river makes
for a great afternoon excursion. If you are interested in a longer
hike, try starting at The Majestic Yosemite Hotel. Although the
lake can be busy in the summer, this portion of the trail sees
comparatively little foot traffic. Finally, if you are a triathlon sort
of family, you could easily ride bikes from Half Dome Village to
the trailhead, hike from there and enjoy a chilly swim at the lake.
Just an idea for you really hard-core types!

Mirror Lake has a lot of places for kids to splash in the water.

Distance: 2 miles roundtrip from the marked trailhead or 4 miles roundtrip from The Majestic Yosemite Hotel
Elevation gain: Negligible
Time: 1 or 2 hours, plus play time!
Starting point: For the shortest hiking distance, begin at the Mirror Lake Trailhead. We highly recommend riding the free shuttle to stop #17, or having a nonhiking member of your party drop you off. While you can try to use it, the parking area closest to the trailhead is quite often full during the peak summer season and adds another three-quarters of a mile total to your hike.

As you head out from the trailhead, you may feel as if you have joined a pilgrimage. People of all sorts are alongside you, anticipating the cool, clear waters of Mirror Lake, which is really just a wide, slow spot in Tenaya Creek. Don't let the sheer numbers deter you—there is room for all at the destination, and the crowded hike is well worth it. The trail winds through shaded, deciduous forest and up and down small rises. It is pleasant and mostly cool as you hike along the creek in places. If you feel at some point that anyone in your party is overheating, look ahead for a rock overhang along the trail. In those spots, a cold breeze often blows out from between the rocks, which may refresh you.

Continue on, watching the river to your left. Soon rocks begin to block its flow and it widens, creating the "lake." From the trailhead (not the parking area) to where the "lake" begins is about 1 mile. You can choose to pull up at the nearest flat rock, shuck off your shoes, and head in, or you can push on toward the top of the lake and even around to the other side (making the trip 5.5 miles roundtrip). Check on the status of little feet and choose accordingly.

The lake has several lovely, sandy wading areas along the shore, and nice big rocks for sun basking also dot its periphery. The water is nearly numbingly cold, but it feels refreshing on a hot day of hiking. We recommend you make at least a half day of this trip. Come prepared to lay out some beach towels, sit back, and read a book while the kids play by the water. Bring a

Cool off on a hot day in Mirror Lake.

picnic or a hearty snack and just relax. This hike is mostly about enjoying the final destination, so make plans to do just that. Also, even though a lot of other people will likely be hanging out around the lake, there is plenty of room to spread out and claim your own little piece of heaven.

 Mist Trail to Vernal Fall

This highly exciting and challenging hike is recommended for capable tweens and teens who like adventure.

Distance: 2.4 miles roundtrip
Elevation gain: 1000 feet
Time: 3 hours
Starting point: Begin the hike from the Happy Isles parking area, or shuttle stop #16 if you can't find a close parking spot.

Hikers climbing the stairs to Vernal Fall

This bridge is fun as a viewpoint, but this spot is too dangerous for water play.

Because this parking area is the starting point for a lot of the Half Dome hikers who leave before first light and are gone the entire day, there is little turnover of parking spots. We highly recommend using the shuttle buses to arrive here or have a nonhiking member of your group drop you off.

The trailhead is also very close to the Upper Pines Campground, so if you are staying there, you might check into the shortest walk to the trailhead from your campsite.

When we began researching our trip to Yosemite, we knew we needed to take our teenagers up this trail. It offers them challenge, adventure, and the thrill of a little danger. If you come prepared, you and your older kids can have an amazing experience.

The hike begins along a paved path that heads steeply uphill. There are likely tons of people heading toward the first attraction, the footbridge, at about 0.8 mile. The trail to the footbridge climbs steadily upward for the first 400 feet of elevation gain. There are some neat features along the way, including a spring with a manmade pool at the base, great for soaking feet on the way down. Also, on this trail you will cross a footbridge that offers picturesque views back out toward the Valley and up toward your destination, Vernal Fall. The water is cold and fast, and people drown here every year. This is not an ideal spot to wade and cool your feet. Just wait—you will be wetter and cooler than you can imagine shortly. There is a sometimes-working bathroom here but no drinking water.

Continuing up the hill, you soon come to the divergence of the John Muir Trail and the Mist Trail to Vernal Fall. If you wish to avoid the wet and wild section of the hike to Vernal Fall, take the John Muir Trail, which loops back around after a lot of climbing and switchbacks, making it a much longer but drier route. To continue along the Mist Trail, turn left and start up the stone stairway section.

The stairs are a marvel of human competency and willpower. We were awestruck imagining how difficult it must have been to build those six hundred granite stairs. This section is strenuous but very beautiful, and soon you begin to feel the mist. Keep in mind that *mist* is a romantic word for what is about to hit you. The park service recommends raingear but not umbrellas for this hike. Even though the "mist" is more like a torrential drenching, the wind created by the waterfall would rip an umbrella—and maybe the person holding it—right off the face of the staircase.

As you climb toward the thundering waterfall, the water hitting you increases, and speaking above the sound of it becomes impossible. The beauty and the terror come in waves. Oh, the power of water and nature! There is nothing to do but press on toward the top (well, technically you could always turn back, but somehow you feel you *must* keep going). Eventually the stairs carry you to the side of an immense cliff face. Here the "trail" becomes steps cut out of the cliff wall. There is a railing to hold on to, and this last terrifying push is worth what awaits you at the top.

As you come around the edge of the cliff, you arrive at the top of the falls, where there is an enormous flat area that works well for resting and admiring the view. You can also walk to the rail-enclosed promontory above the falls and feel the fullness of what you have accomplished.

As great as the feeling of accomplishment is, a word of warning is in order. We found the area at the top of Vernal Fall very disappointing. There were two main problems one day we visited. First, the ground squirrels were the most aggressive we have seen. Sadly, they are so used to people feeding them that they will climb right into your day pack while it is on your lap and take your food. We saw many tourists feeding the little animals and trying to get pictures with them on their laps, which is against the park rules posted in this spot and all around the park. Between the animals trying to take our food and the visitors setting a bad example for our kids, the experience at the top was lessened.

The second deterrent to a good time was the activities many of the other guests were engaging in. Feeding the animals was the least of it! People were smoking (both tobacco and harder stuff) and drinking alcohol, and many were very scantily clad. While there is a time and place for most of that, we didn't want our kids to experience it, and we generally don't expect our nature experiences to be subjected to this sort of display.

In the end we spent very little time up top, but we tremendously enjoyed the thrill of the hike itself and highly recommend it to families with teens. Also, the next day we really got a kick out of looking back at the fall from Washburn Point along Glacier Point Road and knowing we had been up there!

 Happy Isles

This respite from the Valley crowds offers an idyllic stroll through a wonderland of islands, bridges, and dappled forest.

The trail to Vernal Fall leads through the mist in the foreground. Be prepared to get wet!

A peaceful trail away from the crowds

Distance: 0.5 mile roundtrip
Elevation gain: None
Time: 30 minutes plus more for exploring nature or the nature center
Starting point: Begin at the Mist Trail Trailhead. If you plan to leave your vehicle in the parking area, you will have a bit of a walk to get to the trailhead. We recommend you take the shuttle to stop #16, which is closest to the trailhead. If you do park, look for one of the two trails that heads east out of the east end of the parking area. Most people take the one that runs alongside the road. The other trail, which cuts through the woods, is lovely, passing many big boulders great for hiding around and climbing on.

A moment of honesty: we had no intention of hiking in Happy Isles. It just sounds so cheesy—contrived, artificial, and out of place with nature and creation. Only our commitment to writing a book that included *all* kid-friendly options pushed us into a place called "Happy Isles." And guess what? It was wonderful!

The braided stream channels create a lot of places to explore.

No kidding. *Wonderful.* People tend to come to Yosemite for big views and big hikes, not peaceful riverside hangouts. We had become extremely stressed out trying to get to all the big views and hikes amid the crowds, and Happy Isles turned out to be just the break we needed.

The trail is paved most of the way and leads through cool, dappled shade to a series of islands, connected by beautiful stone and wood bridges. Even with the low adventure factor and lack of vistas, you really do feel happy here. Among the crowds of the Yosemite Valley, it is heartening to know this wonderfully peaceful place exists.

Various paths run through the trees, but they all meet up—you really can't get lost. Our small kids had a ball running around on paths and over bridges, chasing one another and playing hide-and-seek. At the top end of the second island, when the spring water levels have come down quite a bit, there is a large,

Bridalveil Fall is at the end of a short hike.

shallow, rocky area that is great for kids to wade and play in. Do supervise them, though; the main current of the Merced River can be fast and dangerous.

Also in this area is the Happy Isles Nature Center. It is open only in the summer from 9:30 a.m. to 5:00 p.m., but it is really pretty great. The interesting exhibits caught our kids' attention right away and held it for about thirty minutes. There is also a very tranquil boardwalk through a marshy meadow area called "the Fen" that we loved. We saw a lot of butterflies along the way, and it felt enchanted somehow.

The exhibits in the nature center focus mainly on animals and the habitats found in the immediate area. Animals generally hold our kids' attention longer than displays highlighting history, and the best part about the information in the nature center is that you can walk outside and encounter the four featured ecosystems: forest, talus, river, and fen. Our favorite exhibit was the one about nocturnal animals.

This area would make a great place for younger family members to hang out while an older contingent went up the Mist Trail to Vernal Fall. If your family is like ours, toddlers and teens and everything in between, then these kinds of strategies are lifesavers. Divide and conquer is how we roll. Use Happy Isles to entertain the younger crowd and the Mist Trail to occupy the older ones, and meet up again here afterward.

 Bridalveil Fall

This short, paved path leads to a majestic Yosemite waterfall that flows all year round—unlike many others.

Distance: 0.5 mile roundtrip
Elevation gain: 100 feet
Time: 20 minutes
Starting point: Begin at the Bridalveil Fall parking area, 6.9 miles west of the visitor center (see Glacier Point Region Map)

The short, paved path begins from the parking area. Follow it toward the sound of the 617-foot-tall waterfall. Along the path you will encounter boulders that are fun to scramble on. Don't rush your kids past them if they want to play. The trail is short enough that you will have plenty of time. Be sure to monitor your kids on the boulders, as the area can be crowded with other people.

When you're ready to move on, head to the viewing area for the falls. There is not much to do besides look at it, but kids may enjoy the spray on their skin in hot weather.

 Lower Yosemite Fall

You can't miss this wide, paved path that attracts crowds of people. The destination is worth fighting the crowds.

Distance: 1.1 miles
Elevation gain: Negligible
Time: 45 minutes
Starting point: Lower Yosemite Fall Trailhead at shuttle stop #6, west of the visitor center and east of the Yosemite Valley Lodge. It is possible to hike from either the visitor center or the lodge to the base of the fall.

As you start out you cross a stream on a log bridge, which small children may enjoy. Shortly after the bridge, you come to the bathroom area. Beyond that it is a straight, short walk to the fall. You can catch glimpses of it from the path, so don't forget to look up every once in a while. Kids will be able to get close enough to feel the mist if the fall is going strong. Remember that as tall as this lower fall looks, there is another one above it that you won't be able to see from here!

To make this little trail part of a larger trip, add it as a spur off the Sentinel and Cooks Meadow Loop. That trail passes right by the Lower Yosemite Fall Trailhead. See below for details.

Opposite: Kids love waterfalls like Lower Yosemite Fall. (Photo by Katie Grullón)

The trail to Yosemite Falls is crowded but provides views of the upper and lower falls.

These meadows are flat, but the surrounding countryside sure isn't!

 ## Sentinel and Cooks Meadow Loop

This peaceful loop features views of Yosemite Falls and Half Dome.

Distance: 2.25 miles roundtrip
Elevation gain: None
Time: 1–2 hours
Starting point: The most common approach is to get on Southside Drive heading east (the only direction you can go on this road) until you see the sign for Swinging Bridge. At this point, take any parking spot along the road wide enough to accommodate your car. If you haven't found a spot by the time you get to Sentinel Bridge, turn left across the bridge and try elsewhere. Alternatively, you could start at the parking area for Lower Yosemite Fall or the Yosemite Valley Lodge, which are both situated along the trail.

This trail is a combination walking and biking trail. If you are a pedestrian, especially a pedestrian with offspring, keep a sharp eye out for bicyclists. This slow-paced walk has multiple views of two of the Valley greats: Yosemite Falls and Half Dome. The meadows themselves are gorgeous to walk through, especially in early spring when the grasses are green and the wildflowers are blooming. Wildlife, particularly deer, are abundant in the mornings and early evenings.

 Four Mile Trail

We recommend this hike as a one-way trip from the top down!

Distance: 4.5 miles one way
Elevation gain: 3200 feet
Time: 3–5 hours one way
Starting point: Glacier Point is recommended, but the Valley end of the trail is at the Four Mile Trailhead between Sentinel Beach and Swinging Bridge.

See the Glacier Point Region Hiking Adventures section for a full trip report and recommendations.

Adventures beyond Hiking

Although we have already outlined some basic options for adding adventure to your trip, here we give you some further options for the Valley region specifically. As you plan your time here, consider adding one or more of the following experiences.

Boating

At times when the roads and parking areas are clogged and congested, the beautiful Merced River boasts plenty of space and a delightful pace at which to view the falls and promontories of the Valley walls. While much of the water in Yosemite is fast flowing and dangerous, the Merced through the Valley floor is tranquil and calm. The waters are still frigid snowmelt, but the experience is worth it. Until you have experienced it, it can be hard to imagine the peace that washes over you as you step off

Visitors along the Merced River (Photo by Katie Grullón)

terra firma into a boat and float away from the hectic pace of land dwellers. Not to mention the joy kids experience as they get to float, splash, and rock along. What a fantastic way to soak up the views of the Valley walls!

Boating with kids requires some added planning and precautions. You need to consider the cold and wet conditions, how to protect them from exposure, and what gear you and your

Floating the Merced River offers families a fresh perspective on the Valley. (Carol M. Highsmith's America Project, Library of Congress)

children will need to help you accomplish that goal. Taking the time to mitigate the negative effects of these elements may make the difference between the best family memory or the worst outdoor experience ever.

This water will be cold, as it is flowing out of the high country as snowmelt. Kids of all ages tend to get grouchy quickly when they are cold. Even on a hot day, they can go from complaining about being too hot to crying about being too cold in an instant. Keeping young ones warm around cold water can be difficult, but it is not impossible. First, consider your boat type. An open inner tube will mean wet feet and bottoms and exposure to the cool air coming off the surface of the water. Although an inner tube can be wildly fun at a water park or on a warm river, it may not be the best choice here. A raft with a floor will keep your children insulated slightly from the water. Exercising care while entering and exiting the boat can also keep little feet dry and therefore warmer.

Another trick we use is to have our kids wear wool socks. The wool socks of today are entirely different from the thick, itchy things of the past. For a very affordable price, you can purchase comfortable wool socks for kids. Of course, they can be worn hiking, but you can also wear them inside sandals, water shoes, or even a pair of old tennis shoes while boating. Wool will help keep wet feet warmer because it insulates even when wet. Finally, make sure you have a dry sweatshirt or some long fleece pants at the end of the trip to warm up cold kids fast. For more specifics on this topic, refer to the gear recommendations in Weather and How to Prepare for It.

The park has established official rules to keep people safe and the environment protected. Some of these rules apply to boaters everywhere in the park and some apply only to the Valley area. The section you will want to consider rafting is the Merced River from Stoneman Bridge to El Capitan Bridge. This is novice-rated water (class I–II) and therefore manageable for beginners. Park rules require that all children thirteen years and younger wear a personal flotation device (PFD, formerly "life vest") at all times while on the water. All other boaters must at least carry a PFD; however, we recommend that every person wear one while on the water. Unexpected events can arise, and you may not have time or you may be too cold to get a PFD on in a hurry. This recommendation becomes a hard rule when the water levels are high.

Before entering the water anywhere in the park, check in with a ranger so that you know current conditions and warnings. Often a storm in the higher elevations, unseen to Valley visitors, can create a sudden flood situation. A ranger will be able to tell you whether or not it is a good day to hit the water.

Next you need to be sure you are accessing the water at approved locations. Trying to enter or exit the water in unapproved areas causes damage to the streamside and its riparian habitat and can also be dangerous to you and your family. Access points in the section from Stoneman Bridge to El Capitan Bridge are as follows: the 100-foot section downstream from the Stoneman Bridge (or as signed); the sandy area devoid of vegetation called Sentinel Beach, downstream from Swinging Bridge; and the area approximately 100 feet upstream and also downstream of El Capitan Bridge. These locations provide safe access for launching and removing boats.

Once you've confirmed that it's a good day to brave the water, you can rent boats from a few locations in the Valley. They have their own restrictions, including no children weighing less than fifty pounds on a rental boat, number of people per boat, and number of capable paddlers (a person at least five feet tall and at least twelve years old). Make sure you consult their rules and regulations before your trip in case your family won't meet their requirements—it would be very disappointing to find that out the morning of your planned water adventure. For more information on rafting see Resources.

You also have the option of bringing your own watercraft to the park. At this point Yosemite does not inspect personal watercraft, but you should make sure your watercraft is clean and dry when you arrive so as not to accidentally introduce any invasive aquatic species. You are also responsible for ensuring that your craft is in good working condition. You might consider bringing small rafts, canoes, inflatable kayaks, inner tubes, or stand-up paddleboards (SUPs). If you need to rent PFDs or paddles, check with the boat rental agency at one of their various locations. They are happy to help you with those items.

Remember, the river only flows one way! If your entire party wants to float, you will need to arrange a way to get back to your car. The rental boat shuttle buses are happy to take you for a minimal per-person fee, provided your deflated watercraft fits on your laps. If you have a SUP, check to see if the buses can accommodate you. Remember, you can always pay for just one adult to ride back to the parking lot and have that person drive back to pick up the rest of the crew. This approach saves money and will accommodate larger watercraft.

Bicycling

In many national parks, bikes are prohibited on trails. Since activities in the parks revolve around hiking the trails, finding a good spot to bike with kids can be challenging—not so in Yosemite Valley! While bikes are prohibited on hiking trails in Yosemite, as in other national parks, a gem of a riding trail encircles nearly the entire Valley floor (see map below). Pedaling two wheels is a wonderful way to take in the big sights and let kids release energy. There is no appreciable elevation gain. Some of the best views of the popular attractions can be appreciated from the 12-mile path around Sentinel and Cooks Meadows. We highly recommend either bringing or renting kids' bikes and then making your way along the path. The adults can ride or walk, and strollers are also welcome here! Biking is a great way to avoid the road-clogging traffic.

Rent from a few locations in the Valley, on a first-come, first-served basis. You'll find them at Half Dome Village (shuttle stop #13)

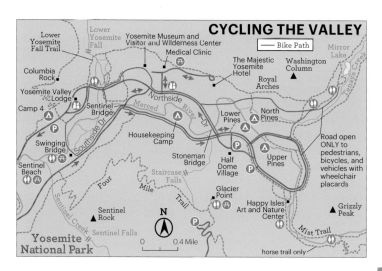

next to the front office and Yosemite Valley Lodge (shuttle stop #8) near the pool. The following are a few rules to keep in mind. Children under eighteen years of age are required to wear a helmet, although riders of all ages are strongly encouraged to do so. Also, only one person per bike is allowed—not even babies in baby carriers are permitted. (You can, however, rent a wheeled attachment called a "tag-along," which attaches onto the front or back of the bike.) Teach your kids before your trip to ride single file and how to alert pedestrians to their approach and passing.

We can't encourage you strongly enough to consider a biking trip around the Valley. It seemed like such a hassle to bring or rent bikes that we didn't really plan on doing any biking. Once we got there and realized how crowded the roads and parking areas were, we decided that biking should have been our number one priority! You may never get a chance to bike in such an idyllic setting, and biking is usually a great activity for kids. Take the opportunity to have a great biking experience in a stunning setting!

Fishing

Because of the abundant waterfalls on most of Yosemite's larger streams, native fish were historically found only in the lower elevations of the park. However, beginning in the late 1800s, rainbow trout were stocked in most every lake and stream in the park, a practice that continued until 1990. The holdovers from these efforts are still available to anglers today, although the fish in nine specific high-country lakes have been removed to allow native amphibians that were being harmed by the non-native fish to recover. Check the park's fishing regulations for more detailed information.

The best fishing in Yosemite is found in the high-country lakes and streams along Tioga Road and in the Tuolumne Meadows area. In the Yosemite Valley there is good fishing in the Merced River, particularly the downstream sections farther from the crowds and campsites where there can be a lot

Big views inspire big smiles at Glacier Point.

of people playing in the water. Another overlooked option is Tenaya Creek for the 2.5 miles upstream from where it joins the Merced. You'll want to avoid the crowded Mirror Lake area for fishing, but fewer people venture upstream from there.

Services and Amenities

This area provides all the services you could need, apart from a gas station. Yosemite Village has a medical clinic, wilderness center, visitor center, post office, convenience store, gift shop, restaurants, and the park's headquarters facilities.

GLACIER POINT REGION

Although the Glacier Point area is located so close to the Yosemite Valley that many might consider it merely an extension of the Valley, we consider it its own region because it has an entirely different atmosphere. And while many of the activities here relate to sights in the Valley, they truly offer a distinctive experience. We hope that you consider spending some time relaxing here with your kids, high above the Valley floor, while in Yosemite.

Things You Need to Know

Glacier Point refers to both a region and a specific location. The actual point is at the terminus of Glacier Point Road and offers stunning views of the Valley from a higher vantage. Glacier Point Road cuts through this region, and all of the main hiking adventures originate from it. The road branches off Wawona Road (State Route 41) as it heads north into the park from the South Entrance. The turnoff to the Yosemite Ski and Snowboard Area (formerly Badger Pass Ski Area) is the point at which the road closes in winter. They keep it plowed just to the turnoff, but typically by May you can head all the way out to Glacier Point and its stellar views. Also remember during your planning that Glacier Point Road can be quite a drive from the Valley or from campgrounds off Big Oak Flat Road to the opposite side of the Valley. The park estimates that it takes around an hour to drive from the Valley floor to Glacier Point, but it can take substantially longer during peak hours, morning and evening. Plan accordingly.

While most people head to this area to gaze out over the Valley from the popular Glacier Point, we want to encourage you to think a little differently. Remember, even though kids are generally unimpressed with views, we encourage you to think about experiencing a few of the lesser-known features of this area to engage them in ways that they will appreciate. If the crowds and craze of the Valley have you stressed out and the nature experience you were hoping for hasn't materialized, this area may be the respite you need. Aside from the actual Glacier Point, relatively few people are out of their cars and exploring on foot here, giving you the chance to experience some peace and quiet and a slower pace. Read some of our hiking

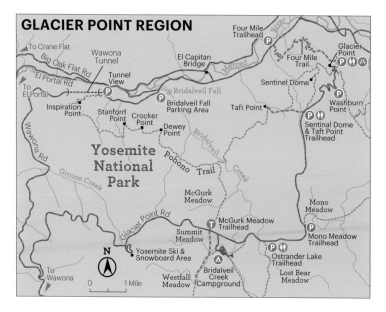

GLACIER POINT REGION

Yosemite National Park

suggestions below and plan some time to explore Glacier Point. You will be glad you did.

As for helping kids enjoy the views that we adults always seem to crave, be sure to visit the Valley area at the beginning of your Yosemite trip. Kids will enjoy the views from Glacier Point much more if they can find sights they have already hiked to or around. They will be willing to engage in the experience longer if you help them pinpoint places they have already been. Also consider bringing binoculars for them to use here. They will have great fun looking at all the "ant people" hiking, biking, and driving below them and especially the hikers along the cables section of Half Dome, across the chasm of the Valley floor. Giving kids who are old enough a camera to use—either a disposable one or a cheap digital model—also invites deeper engagement with the views before them.

Hiking Adventures

While many of the well-known hikes here are little more than a stroll to an overlook, we have rounded up a few other options to get your kids excited.

 Four Mile Trail

A strenuous trail any way you hike it, but an amazing experience for older, experienced hikers.

Distance: 4.5 miles one way (recommended, see below)
Elevation loss: 3200 feet
Time: 3–5 hours, plus time for shuttle if going one way
Starting point: Begin at Glacier Point if you're heading down, or from the Four Mile Trailhead along Southside Drive in the Yosemite Valley if you're heading up.

The Four Mile Trail cuts steeply from the heights of Glacier Point down to the Yosemite Valley, taking in all the sights on the north side of the Valley along the way. It is steep, rocky, and exposed—a marvelous adventure. We highly recommend taking the paid tour bus from the Valley to Glacier Point and hiking down. While the views may sometimes be to your back when hiking in this direction, it will be a much more manageable distance when going downhill. There is no direction to hike in that will lessen the "strenuous" ranking of this hike, but you'll breathe easier if you are going downhill! Remember that going downhill can be very stressful on quadriceps, knees, and ankles, so consider your own needs as necessary. If you decide to take the shuttle one way, look into current schedules and pricing at www.travelyosemite.com and click on their guided bus tours under "Things to Do." If the tour is too pricey for your whole family, consider sending one adult back up on the bus to retrieve your car while the rest of you dip your feet in the Merced River.

The views of Half Dome from Glacier Point are spectacular.

Now, as for the hike itself, the trail is wide and smooth and easy to find, as this is one of the more popular hikes from this area. Just follow the trail as it goes down, down, down. In the top section you will be able to see views of Clouds Rest, North Dome, Half Dome, and up Tenaya Canyon. Continuing down you will see Cathedral Rocks and El Capitan framing a reverse tunnel view. A mile or so from the bottom you will be able to see Yosemite Falls from top to bottom. Most other views of Yosemite Falls only let you see it a portion at a time, but on this hike you will get to see it all. Remember that these falls don't run all year long, so if seeing them is on your bucket list, this hike is best done earlier in the summer when they are still running strong. As you hit the final section of the trail you will enter the timber that covers the lower slopes and the views will fade. Still, you may be thankful for the shade and the fact that you are almost to the bottom.

If you want even more information about this hike, visit one of our favorite online sources for hiking information: www.yosemitehikes.com.

Taft Point

This is a fun-filled hike to "the fissures," a geologic curiosity, offering a stunning drop-off view of the Valley.

Distance: 2.2 miles roundtrip
Elevation gain: 200 feet
Time: 1–2 hours
Starting point: Begin at the Sentinel Dome and Taft Point Trailhead on Glacier Point Road. If the parking area on the northwest side of the road is full, use a spot on the side of the road. Your trail will be heading off to the west, so park west of the parking area if possible.

This is by far our favorite hike in this region; it even garners a spot in our top five hikes in this park! Not only that but it was great for every member of our family, ranging from age four to adult. Few hikes can boast such a wide appeal!

Although the parking location is clear, it can be difficult to determine the exact trail you will follow. That is partly due to the many social trails that leave from various parts of the parking and bathroom area and partly because the trail up Sentinel Dome leaves from here also. Your trail leads to the west, while Sentinel Dome is visible to the northeast. Take the most obvious trail to the west and stay left at any forks, and you will soon find the dedicated trail.

Shortly after leaving the split that leads to Sentinel Dome, you come to a copse of trees. The trail is mostly rolling here and very pleasant. Shortly after entering the trees you arrive at a small creek crossing, an excellent spot to let small children stop and play. Our group split up here: the older group hiked on and the four-year-old stayed behind with an adult to enjoy the water.

The rambling trail continues across the creek and in and out of groups of trees. There are a lot of rocks that are perfect for hopping and scrambling. While the prevalence of granite in Yosemite can mean a lack of flora, there is a lot of plant life in this area, including gorgeous wildflowers in the spring months.

The views at the end of the trail to Taft Point are the icing on the cake of an all-around great hike.

Expect to see an ever-changing display of flowers as the season progresses. Early in spring you might be lucky enough to find the seemingly artificial red top of a waxy snow flower shooting up through snow. These flowers do not carry out photosynthesis; instead, they get their energy from fungi in the soil. Hummingbirds feed on the bell-shaped flowers. After the snow flowers fade, look for red columbine, Sierra forget-me-nots, monkeyflowers, and mountain pennyroyal to name a few.

Our kids enjoyed running this trail, hopping rocks, and feeling the wind in their faces. The trail is gradual enough that kids should be able to avoid wipeouts. Usually they will

When you see the railing, you will know you are almost there.

self-regulate on how fast they run based on their confidence and ability levels.

Eventually you will come to a wide area that may be boggy and require some maneuvering to cross (in spring and fall). Then you come to a rocky, boulder-strewn area that leads down to an open area populated with large, flat boulders.

As you head out onto the flat, rocky surface, Taft Point is in the near distance, with people spread out over the area between. The trail is less obvious on this hard, dry surface, but you also have much less risk of harming plant life by being off-trail. Do your best to make your way toward Taft Point. Although the view of the point beckons you on, don't miss the fissures on the way!

These huge cracks in the cliff face are off to the right of the trail. Some fissures are wide and others are narrow like slot canyons. Some are boulder choked, and some give you unobstructed views hundreds of feet down. The fissures is a popular place for slacklining, which we like to watch but don't indulge in ourselves. Our kids got a big kick out of seeing people doing that death-defying feat. Whether the slackliners are there or not, take time to check out the fissures before heading to Taft Point.

As you head slightly uphill from the fissures toward Taft Point, an area with a guardrail at the tip of a huge rock outcropping comes into view. This is the official Taft Point. It really is a bit terrifying to stand there and look down at the Valley floor—even with a guardrail! However, if you can overcome a bit of vertigo, there is no better way to look down on the Valley than from the lofty height of 3000 feet. You can also catch a breathtaking view of the upper portion of Yosemite Falls here. Our big kids loved the easy hike to a big-thrills viewpoint. If you want a few good photo ops of your very responsible, trustworthy older kids, you can leave them at the point and head back toward the fissures. Photo ops abound on the outcropping with the cliff dropping away in the background. There is also a dramatic photo spot to the left, a bit west from Taft Point, where your subjects appear to be perched on a seemingly fragile rock suspended above the river valley below. Please try these shots only with kids you know will practice wisdom and restraint around cliffs. Always keep your little and impulsive imps by your side and within hand-holding distance.

After you have satisfied your need to stare death in the face, head away from the cliff edge and back the way you came. Pick up any creekside stragglers and return to the car. If you are thirsty for more hiking, you could hit Sentinel Dome here. We don't review it because it is a very exposed hike with a steep ascent to views that aren't any better than others you can get in the area. Our kids aren't much for that sort of thing, and yours probably aren't either. However, it is an option if you just need more to do!

Watching our kids on this point gave us butterflies, but they loved it.

Westfall Meadow

This trail is tricky to find, and therefore seldom used, making it a tranquil spot to enjoy meadow vistas. It may not provide big thrills, but it offers solitude, nature, and maybe a snowball fight.

Distance: Up to 2.8 miles roundtrip to the meadow and back
Elevation gain: 100 feet
Time: 1.5–2.5 hours
Starting point: There is no official parking area for this trail, but look for the "McGurk Meadow" sign on the north side of the road, after the ski area turnoff but just before the turnoff to Bridalveil Creek Campground. The gravel shoulder fits about three cars. Park here. If these spots are filled, park anywhere you can find a wide spot in the road and walk back to the trailhead.

From the recommended parking area, look to the south side of the road, across from the "McGurk Meadow" sign, and spot the faint trail heading south from the road. Cross carefully and head up the trail.

Shortly after climbing the embankment and tentatively heading down an unmarked trail, you come to a metal sign with the trail name that will let you know you've come to the right place. You will also see a sign that says "Permits required" with a bunch of other information. At first you may think you are no longer allowed to hike here, but rest assured, the sign is addressing the need for permits to camp in the backcountry, not to hike. As long as you plan to come back out the same day you are hiking in, you don't need a permit.

After hiking through the trees for a bit, you emerge onto a big, flat, stone area that makes reading the trail difficult. Look for rock cairns, which the park service and some well-meaning hikers stack to point the way. By the way, our kids love to stack rocks along the trail. They like to see how many they can balance, always in more challenging arrangements than have been made before. As long as they create them along the trail, it is a pretty harmless way to "leave our mark," as we

Moving water and downed trees may be enough to pique your children's interest.

humans seem inclined to do. It doesn't mar the natural beauty
of a place and can be dispersed easily with a swipe of a stick.
Since they are used as official trail markers in certain places,
please don't let your children build them off-trail, which could
confuse hikers passing through here after you.

In this area you can find the trail location by imagining this
large, rocky area to be almost square shaped. You are entering
on the lower left corner, and the trail continues from the upper
right-hand corner. Look that direction and you should see the

rock cairns pointing the way. Follow the trail back into the alpine forest.

After about two-thirds of a mile you come to the old Glacier Point Road, overgrown and gravelly but still recognizable as a road. Here the road goes left toward Bridalveil Creek Campground, and another trail heading off to the right leads to Summit Meadow. After a possible small creek crossing, depending on the season, continue straight, roughly following the creek that trickles past on your left. It was here in the trees that we found little pockets of snow remaining and had ourselves an energetic snowball fight. You won't find snow into August here, but in the spring, through mid-June, you very likely will.

Eventually you come out at the foot of the meadow. Although you can continue on around the meadow, there isn't much more to be gained from a kid's perspective. Meadows are important but fragile ecosystems—do not tramp through them. Plus, they often have wet, boggy areas that don't announce themselves. If your crew does want to extend the hike, walking on the periphery of the meadow is the best option. Meadows can be great places to spot wildlife.

After you have had your fill of unspoiled nature with few to no other visitors, head back out the way you came. A final note: we do recommend bug repellent for this hike. Small creeks and meadows often have large populations of pesky insects, and you and your little ones will enjoy the hike much more if the bugs are kept at bay.

If you enjoyed Westfall Meadow and would like more of the same, McGurk Meadow, across Glacier Point Road from Westfall, is a similar hike. The trail is roughly 1.8 miles roundtrip with around 100 feet of elevation gain. It does have a tiny old log cabin that may or may not make it more interesting than Westfall Meadow. Otherwise it is similar, although possibly more crowded due to the fact the NPS put a location sign for it on the road and include it on its hiking suggestion map.

Washburn Point offers hikers a new perspective on Vernal and Nevada Falls.

Washburn Point

This hike leads to a potentially less crowded viewpoint than Glacier Point with a similar but more easterly view of the Yosemite Valley.

Distance: 0.1 mile or about 20 stair steps
Elevation gain: Negligible except for stairs
Time: 2 minutes
Starting point: Begin at the Washburn Point parking area on Glacier Point Road.

Although this short stroll hardly qualifies as a hike, we have included it because most people will wonder if they should stop for it or just keep going to Glacier Point itself. You should stop. While the views are aimed toward the east end of the Valley, you will get an unforgettable view of Half Dome in profile and Vernal and Nevada Falls. Kids will find this stop especially enjoyable if they have climbed the Mist Trail to the top of Vernal Fall. It is great fun to see that fall from this lofty vantage and realize you climbed it.

The other fun activity for kids here, mentioned earlier, is using a pair of binoculars to watch the people on the ascent of Half Dome. In the later part of the afternoon, you can see a line of people snaking their way along the last and most dangerous part of the climb: the cables. Plan to spend ten to twenty minutes here with the kids. Some wide stone walls and a lot of stone steps make nice places to sit and snack a bit before heading on.

 Glacier Point

While short on action, Glacier Point is long on views and well worth the stop.

Distance: 1 mile roundtrip on pavement
Elevation gain: Negligible
Time: 20–30 minutes, including time to look around
Starting point: The trail begins at the parking area for Glacier Point. Head out to the path beyond the café and bookstore.

Allowing you a head-on look at Yosemite Falls, Glacier Point offers some of the best views anywhere in the park. Half Dome, another view of Vernal and Nevada Falls, North Dome, and the Royal Arches are just a few of the awe-inspiring sights. Sunset here is really stunning as you watch the sunlight slowly leave the canyon. Many people choose to find a rock to sit on just outside the bookstore and enjoy the view from there. You can also hike the (mostly) wheelchair- and stroller-accessible path to a few other vantage points.

Anytime the road is open, you will find crowds. For many visitors, this is the one and only stop on their visit to this region. There are pit-toilet bathrooms around the parking area, but

In this case, views were enough to capture our kids' attention.

expect to find long lines to use them. While crowds generally detract from our family's experience, we still thought it was worth a short stop because of the amazing views.

Adventures beyond Hiking

There are few adventures beyond hiking in this region, which is relatively small and less developed. It is interesting to note that you can ski, tube, and snowboard here in the winter. That's a rarity in national parks, so you may want to consider it.

Services and Amenities

There is a snack shack and gift shop at Glacier Point. They sell souvenirs and food such as sandwiches, baked goods, and ice cream.

TUOLUMNE MEADOWS AND TIOGA ROAD REGION

Sitting at around 8000 feet above sea level, Tuolumne Meadows gives you a very different experience from the Valley floor. Here you will find high alpine meadows punctuated with clear-blue lakes and icy-cold rivers. Granite domes are scattered about the larger meadows, and the air is cooler and fresher than you find in the Valley, which makes hiking to one of the abundant lakes

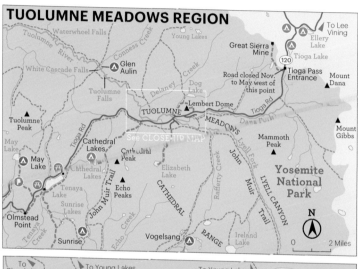

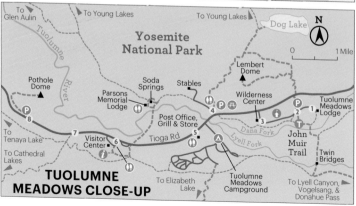

Looking out across Tuolumne Meadows from Lembert Dome

or two groves of giant sequoias a real pleasure. There is plenty to inspire you here in the high country.

Things You Need to Know

The hikes and features we review in this section encompass essentially the entire length of Tioga Road, the main route that transverses the entire park from east to west. This road is closed from November to May due to the large amount of snow that falls in the high country during winter. Starting at the west end of Tioga Road you will find the Tuolumne Grove of Giant Sequoias and its neighbor, Merced Grove (which is technically a few miles up Big Oak Flat Road from its intersection with Tioga Road). The west end of the road is the lowest point, and as you head east you will gain elevation with each twisty curve. If you get stuck behind a motor home here, have patience!

The Tuolumne area had undergone some recent changes at the time of this writing in 2018 that may affect your travel plans. Historically there was a gas station near the Tuolumne Meadows Visitor Center that is now closed, but it still shows up on many maps and reviews of the park. The absence of this gas station means that it is no longer economical for bus operators to service this part of the park, so there are no longer free shuttles to this region. If you want to experience it, you may have to drive there yourself or pay for a shuttle. Check the park's website for the latest updates on bus options (see Resources).

Hiking Adventures

If you came to Yosemite with the desire to get out and stretch your legs on some beautiful trails, this is the place to do it. There are options for short and long hikes with everything in between, but all of the routes in this region deliver breathtaking views. Most of them have something closer at hand for the kids to enjoy as well.

 Lembert Dome

This modest hike takes you to the top of a granite dome with commanding views of the surrounding mountains and valleys. It's our favorite short hike in this region for kids ages six and up. Combine this classic jaunt with Dog Lake (see below) to add some miles to another perfect picnic spot.

Distance: 2.8 miles roundtrip to Lembert Dome
Elevation gain: 850 feet
Time: 2–3 hours
Starting point: Begin at the Dog Lake parking area along the frontage road that leads to Tuolumne Meadows Lodge. Don't be fooled into parking at the Lembert Dome parking and picnic area—it provides a good view of the dome from below, but starting from here will triple the distance to your destination!

The trail leaves from the north side of the parking area and climbs steadily for the first three-quarters of a mile to the trail junction that leads to Lembert Dome. Almost immediately you have to cross busy Tioga Road, so keep a close eye on your little ones as you hurry across.

Enjoy a quick snack while you take in the 360-degree view from Lembert Dome.

The multiple fissures in the rock of Lembert Dome create a choose-your-own-adventure-style hike.

Once you reach the junction, turn left and continue to climb, but at a somewhat reduced incline. You are now on the ridge of the dome, and as you gain elevation, you start to get small tastes of the views ahead as the forest thins and glimpses of the surrounding countryside filter through the trees. Before long you leave the tree line altogether and start walking on a massive slab of granite. Our kids really enjoyed this part because it felt more like bouldering and exploring than simply plodding along a trail, and with the trees gone, you can see your destination ahead and the expanding countryside all around you. The final pitch to the top is actually quite steep and is best approached from the south side.

We found fissures in the granite to act as good footholds for a makeshift trail to the top, and while the pitch was quite steep here in places, we aren't suggesting that this is anywhere close to true rock climbing. If your kids have the slightest taste for adventure, they will love it, and the spectacular views at the top are a great reward for your bravery. You can literally look for miles in every direction from the top of Lembert Dome, and almost everything your eyes see across those vast distances is natural, wild, and sublime.

A word of warning: if storm clouds are threatening, the top of Lembert Dome is not the place to be.

 Dog Lake

This moderate hike heads through the forest to a picturesque lake that makes an excellent picnic spot. But you'll want to bring your insect repellent and/or bug nets because the mosquitoes like it too!

Distance: 4 miles roundtrip
Elevation gain: 750 feet
Time: 3–4 hours
Starting point: Begin at the Dog Lake parking area on the frontage road that leads to Tuolumne Meadows Lodge, or at the Lembert Dome parking and picnic area just off Tioga Road.

This hike along a forested trail to Dog Lake surprised us because the lake is large and in a beautiful setting. If you start from the Lembert Dome parking and picnic area, you will have less elevation gain, but we strongly recommend starting from the Dog Lake parking area and combining it with a side hike to Lembert Dome, one of our favorites in the area.

Once you have reached the junction with the Lembert Dome trail, the bulk of the climbing is behind you, and the terrain from here to the lake is mostly rolling. The main trail delivers you to the west end of the lake, but side trails all around the edge lead to excellent picnic spots where you can soak in the scenery while enjoying a snack and dipping your toes in the refreshing water.

Dog Lake has plenty of shoreline to enjoy good views and a picnic.

 ## Tuolumne Meadows

A pleasant stroll brings you into beautiful Tuolumne Meadows, with stops at Parsons Memorial Lodge and the fascinating Soda Springs, where you can drink natural soda water straight from the earth.

Distance: As much as 2 miles, depending on how far you go

Elevation gain: Negligible

Time: 1–2 hours

Starting point: You have a couple of options. Either park at the visitor center and cross Tioga Road, or park along the road to the stables (past the Dog Lake and Lembert Dome parking on the north side of Tioga Road). We like the approach from the visitor center as it takes you across a bridge over the river—always a winner for kids.

Beautiful Tuolumne Meadows and its namesake river

Whichever point you choose, the way to the trail is clear. The meadow stretches out ahead of you with the gravel trail winding through it. Head across the meadow toward the foothills to the north. As you reach the base of the hills, the trail forks. It becomes a loop, so continuing in either direction is fine. When presented with a choice on direction, consider allowing your children to take turns choosing. This tactic will give them some buy-in—all kids love the chance to be in charge.

Head up the hill and find the historic Parsons Memorial Lodge, built in 1915 by the Sierra Club as a rest spot for hikers. Its name honors one of the club's early directors. The stately stone and wood-beam structure has a library and maps and is often staffed by a ranger or a member of the Sierra Club who is happy to answer questions and tell stories. There are picnic tables outside and a bathroom nearby.

A short walk away from the lodge is Soda Springs, where a small four-sided log structure protects the fragile ground out of which natural soda water bubbles. Pass through the doorway, walking on flat stepping stones, to get a closer look. Kids will be delighted by the bubbling and sputtering mud and water. A sign there describes what you see and gives some historical perspective. You are free to try the soda water at your own risk, remembering that animals also stop here to drink. Being the adventurous sort, we filled a small baggie with some water and enjoyed it on the walk out. All healthy here so far!

Finish off the loop, heading back down to the meadow and walking back out the way you came. Although you may see many people wandering off the path, it is important to protect the fragile alpine-meadow environment. Teach your kids to stay on the trail and explain the reasons why. Invite them into the role of steward and protector of the park, and they will grow to care even more for these wild places.

Natural soda water bubbles up from the earth at Soda Springs.

The one notable exception that the park service makes to this rule concerns the water access around the bridge over the Tuolumne River. Park staff confirmed that wading and swimming on the banks around the bridge is permitted. They did warn, however, that the water is very cold and can be swift. Every year people are swept away to their death in the cold waters of some of Yosemite's creeks, so exercise caution around the water here. Your child may be just as happy throwing rocks and leaf-boats off the bridge.

 Lyell Canyon

Get away from the day crowds and hike along an enchanting river, with multiple bridge crossings and beach areas that will delight your children.

Distance: 1.5 miles or up to 8 miles, depending on when you turn around
Elevation gain: 200 feet over the full length
Time: 1–4 hours, depending on how far you go
Starting point: Begin at either the backcountry permit center (wilderness center) or the Dog Lake parking area. Look for the parking area on the road to the Tuolumne Meadows Lodge, on the south side of Tioga Road. Starting here instead of at the Lembert Dome parking and picnic area will save little legs a mile of walking in the end.

The trail begins downhill and south of the parking area. Follow one of the many social trails to the main trail that hugs the banks of the Dana Fork of the Tuolumne River. If your children are immediately drawn to the water, find an access point and let them enjoy playing on the banks. Shortly you arrive at a bridge that is perfect for throwing stick-boats and rocks into the stream.

After this bridge your trail winds away from the Dana Fork through a drier area. The trail is clear and, even in the peak season, relatively free of people. You will encounter thru-hikers on the John Muir and Pacific Crest Trails or those accessing the

The early sections of the trail up Lyell Canyon hold the most interest for kids.

High Sierra Camps in the area, but the majority of visitors are concentrated in the main Tuolumne Meadows area to the west. At any intersections where your way is in doubt, continue to follow the John Muir and Pacific Crest Trails.

After hiking over a small rise, you drop back down toward Lyell Fork. As you come out of the trees, a grandiose panorama appears: the river, the Twin Bridges, and extraordinary views of the Valley. We could have spent the entire afternoon lounging here! The bridges are constructed of wood and rock to look as though they had just fallen across the huge granite boulders strewn throughout the river. There are plenty of flat spots to picnic on. Take off your shoes and wiggle your toes in the refreshing water. Throw stick-boats upstream and run along watching them catch an eddy or flow over small falls. Of course, watch your children closely any time you are near the water and away from services.

If you choose to leave this small piece of paradise, the trail continues on the other side of the river, crossing the small end of the meadow and heading back into the trees. There are a few trail intersections in this area—just keep to the Pacific Crest and John Muir Trails headed toward Donohue Pass. As the trail winds through the trees, mosquitoes can be annoying, so bug repellent, hats, long pants, and long-sleeved shirts will come in handy.

From this point, you can hike for another 3 miles through the canyon or even farther to Donohue Pass on the edge of the park. Continuing on will be less interesting for small children than staying at the Twin Bridges. Families with older and younger kids may want to separate into groups for their own adventures. The older contingent could hike farther while the younger ones stay at the Twin Bridges with a parent.

Pothole Dome

Even small kids can make their way onto this big dome, giving the whole family a sense of accomplishment.

Distance: 0.25 mile to base of the dome, various routes up the dome, depending on how high you want to climb
Elevation gain: 250 feet
Time: 30 minutes–1 hour
Starting point: Begin at the Pothole Dome parking area, west of the main Tuolumne Meadows area. The trail leaves the parking lot and swings left along the road in order to circumnavigate the meadow. Meadows are strongly susceptible to damage due to human foot-traffic. Keep this meadow pristine by following the main trail around the west end. You will be able to see the entire trail from the parking area.

It's a relatively short hike to this rewarding view from Pothole Dome.

Follow the trail as it loops back to the east along the base of Pothole Dome, a granite monolith. Skirt around the base of the dome to the side that faces out on the meadow to the east. From here people tend to begin ascending the dome from multiple locations. You won't do any damage to the granite, so it is acceptable to make your own way up the rock. The sooner you cut up onto the rock, the steeper the way ahead of you will be. Help your kids resist the urge to get up on the rock as long as possible.

Once you start up the rock, make your way by cutting back and forth toward the top. You are mostly exposed to the elements, so wear sun protection and avoid hiking here if there is a chance of lightning. Hiking in the morning minimizes the chance of both hot sun and thunderstorms. A few sparse trees eke a living out of cracks in the rock, which make for nice spots to stop for water or a snack. If necessary, encourage your kids to keep going although we found that more often, they had to drag us along!

Continue heading up until your kids feel a sense of grown-up accomplishment and the thrill of heights with a grand view. The "pothole" that the rock is named for is found slightly toward the road side of the dome. The top area is fairly flat, a good spot for some play time. Evaluate your children's abilities and supervise them accordingly.

When you have exhausted the fun, head back down the dome. Taking a back-and-forth path lessens the strain on your knees and ankles. Our kids pretended they were skiing a slalom course! When you reach the base, return to the parking area along the trail.

 ## Gaylor Lakes

This short but steep climb leads to a high alpine basin dotted with several lakes and an abandoned mine site.

Distance: 1 mile to the first lake
Elevation gain: 500 feet
Time: 1.5–2.5 hours
Starting point: The trailhead, which sits at 10,000 feet of elevation, is accessible from the parking area just inside the Tioga Pass Entrance.

Starting high, this trail climbs even higher quickly for the majority of the route. The steep, rocky trail is one of the more difficult climbs that we experienced in the park. But as you reach the top of the ridge, the vistas are very rewarding, so see if your family is willing to hike primarily for the view. If so, this could make your list of great hikes.

You can look farther up into the basin and see the various lakes in the large alpine bowl that you may feel like visiting if you have any breath left. From the ridge you drop down two hundred feet to the shores of Middle Gaylor Lake. We stopped

Middle Gaylor Lake sits in a beautiful alpine bowl.

here to cool our feet in the frigid water while another family nearby kept busy catching and releasing a few trout. There are plenty of places to relax along the shores of the lake, take in the scenery, and observe wildflowers. Being short on time, this is as far as we went, but the trail continues farther up the valley for another mile through the basin to the slopes of Gaylor Peak, eventually ending at the old Great Sierra Mine site. This area has some open mine shafts, so use caution if you go there with your children.

 ## Elizabeth Lake

This hike has a great payoff for a moderate effort. It ends at a stunning, glacier-carved basin that has multiple water courses, with the namesake lake beautifully reflecting Unicorn Peak.

Few places are more picturesque than the basin that holds Elizabeth Lake.

Distance: 4.8 miles roundtrip, out and back
Elevation gain: 1000 feet
Time: 4–5 hours
Starting point: This hike begins at the back of Tuolumne Meadows Campground Loop B. As you enter the campground, turn right and follow the main driveway through the campground for perhaps a third of a mile, then turn uphill toward the horse camping area. The trailhead is near the bathrooms for the horse camp.

This trail may require a bit of patience because it starts with a fair, though not excessive, amount of climbing. Furthermore, the initial section lies in a pretty forest, but it does not provide much in terms of broad views or great distractions for children. If you stick with it, eventually you see a creek approaching the trail on the right side, as well as trails down to the shore. The views from here are nice, and we enjoyed a break by the stream,

but we later wished we had pushed just a little farther before stopping, because the views and water features just got better and better a short way up the trail.

As you near the lake, you first enter a beautiful alpine meadow, which can be quite marshy in places earlier in the summer. Kids don't mind a little mud on their boots, so continue on until you reach a junction of two small streams, one from Elizabeth Lake and the other descending from the alpine basin to your left and south. There are lakes at the head of this stream as well, but we have not visited them. At this point you have several options in terms of trails. The main trail follows the stream to the left but then seems to split up and peter out in spots. We followed it for a while until we found a narrow spot in the creek, then jumped across so that we could make our way over to the shores of Elizabeth Lake. A network of social trails covers this area; pick one out that heads in the general direction you want to go and see where it leads—there are no bad options. The lake is beautiful, the backdrop, dazzling, picnic spots, abundant, and there are plenty of places for your kids to enjoy playing in and around the water.

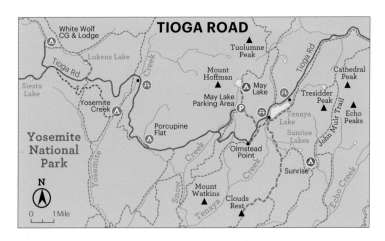

 Tenaya Lake

Spending time at the beach area and hiking the backside of Tenaya Lake were among our favorite experiences in this park. We highly recommend it.

Distance: 2.5 mile loop (not recommended) or 1 mile hiking only one direction along the southeast side (opposite the road)
Elevation gain: Negligible
Time: 1–2 hours
Starting point: Begin from either end of Tenaya Lake in the picnic and parking areas.

Some websites and even some rangers in the park will tell you that this is a loop "trail." While you can walk the entire distance around Lake Tenaya, much of that walking will be on the shoulder of Tioga Road—unpleasant and quite dangerous

One of the many views of Tenaya Lake along this trail

with children. Our recommendation for family members who prefer hiking to beach-bumming is to have them go on a hike around the far side of the lake that ends at the beach. Have the beach contingent drop the hikers at the southwest end of the lake, and they can then drive along Tioga Road to park near the big sandy beach at the easternmost end. This group can get set up with some beach towels, toys, and a snack to hang out while they wait for the hiking group.

For the hikers, you will be starting off from one of the parking lots on the southwest end of the lake. The trail starts along the same trail as other popular area hikes (Clouds Rest and Sunrise Lakes). Find the trail and follow it to a large, sandy river crossing. Flat rocks placed across may assist you, but they are often underwater, in which case you will need to remove your shoes and wade across.

Massive granite formations make up the backdrop to May Lake.

After crossing the creek, head left to follow the shore of the lake. The other trails will branch off, but you want to continue to hug the shoreline. All along this part of the trail you have phenomenal views back across the lake to the granite domes rising above the water. The clouds, the sky, the water, and the mountains conspire to create one of the most breathtaking views in this end of the park.

Continuing around the lake, the trail sometimes rises slightly above the shoreline and sometimes drops back to meet it. Enjoy the mostly level terrain and phenomenal sights along the way. As you get closer to the sandy-beach end of the lake, the trail seems to split. To get back to your family or return to Tioga Road, continue to stay close to the shore. The trail quickly dumps you onto the beach. Head toward the road and encounter another creek crossing, this time of the outlet stream. After crossing the stream on the available logs, you are on the main beach, where you can reunite with your family and enjoy some time on the beach.

If you are following the loop instead of the recommended one-way route, join up with Tioga Road and follow it back around the lake. The road bends out around the picnic area about halfway back. About half of the trip has a sidewalk, and then you have to walk on the shoulder of the road for the rest. It is long, hot, and slightly dangerous.

 **May Lake**

Another stunning lake accessed via a relatively short hike, this trail is very popular for a good reason.

Distance: 2.4 miles roundtrip, out and back
Elevation gain: 500 feet
Time: 2–3 hours roundtrip
Starting point: Access this trail from the May Lake parking area at the end of the side road that leaves from Tioga Road, a few miles west of Olmstead Point and Tenaya Lake.

Take in this panorama while you catch your breath.

You'll likely have company on this short hike to a gorgeous lake. Beginning at the west side of the parking lot, the trail weaves alongside a shallow pond and then starts to climb, moderately at first. This trail has some tree cover but is mostly open as it crosses over a large bench of fractured granite slabs. After about two-thirds of the way, the trail starts to gain elevation in earnest, but you can use the climb as an opportunity to stop and look back at the amazing views as you catch your breath. Your kids may also need encouragement in the way of a quick energy-boosting snack. Take in the views while you recharge, and then keep heading up.

As you reach the top of the steep section, the vistas back to the south are vast, and you'll have the satisfaction of knowing your destination is not too far ahead.

The shores of the lake are actually the location of a High Sierra Camp that can be reserved for overnight stays, so there are a few facilities here, including pit toilets, water spigots, and bear boxes. As you reach the lake and approach the shore, look across a large body of crystal-blue water that reflects Mount Hoffman. This massive formation of granite is impressive to behold, and there are no fewer than three waterfalls cascading down the far side of the lake, depending on the season and moisture level. Trails lead you down either side of the lake to many different picnic and resting spots. It may look tempting, but swimming is prohibited in May Lake because it is used for drinking water. If you want to explore further, you can scramble up the granite faces on the far side of the lake in any number of places.

Finally, we chose to split up our older and younger children on this hike. After dropping off Dad and the older kids at the trailhead, Mom and the younger set drove back down the road and enjoyed relaxing at the beaches on the west end of Tenaya Lake. The older boys hiked from the May Lake parking area down the trail that leads to Tenaya Lake. To find this route, leave from the north end of the parking area and follow a broad trail that was an access road about one hundred years ago. This trail is downhill the whole way to Tenaya Lake, so it is an easy way to get some more miles in without too much effort.

 Lukens Lake

This short hike takes you to a nice little lake that borders one of the prettiest alpine meadows we've ever seen. With a shaded trail and a lake warm enough for a quick dip, it is an excellent choice on a warm day.

Distance: 1.8 miles roundtrip
Elevation gain: 200 feet
Time: 1.5–2 hours

Lukens Lake adjoins a gorgeous meadow with spectacular wildflowers if you catch it in season.

Starting point: There are two ways to get here. We recommend that you start at the Lukens Lake Trailhead parking area on Tioga Road, slightly east of the turnoff to White Wolf Campground. You can also start from the campground itself, but that turns it into a 5.4-mile roundtrip hike.

Suitable for nearly any family, this hike has some features that make it especially attractive to younger kids right from the start. From the parking lot on the south side of Tioga Road, you first cross the road and immediately enter a forest. Here the trail winds around and crosses a shallow stream a couple of times. The presence of this amount of water is always a draw for younger kids, and the large number of gigantic fallen Douglas firs scattered about in this area proves captivating as well. In some cases, the standing snags are hollowed out, making for fun natural jungle gyms for your kids to climb up, over, and through. The creek is also small enough to splash in and perhaps float a stick-boat or two. If you are looking for a nice, shaded picnic spot in a natural setting, this would be a great place to find one just fifty yards off the road.

From here the trail starts to gain elevation, but at a reasonable rate. You quickly reach the top of the ridge and then start down toward the lake, with good tree cover the entire way. As you near the lake, a charming meadow comes into view on your right. When we were there in late July, lupine, cow parsnip, and Henderson's shooting star (to name a few) carpeted the ground in a colorful wildflower display. To say it was picturesque would be an understatement—we couldn't stop taking photos of this beautiful spot.

On the far side of the meadow lies the lake, but the meadow itself can be quite marshy. Protect your feet and the meadow by staying on the trail. In a short while you reach the edge of the lake. It was shallow enough on one of our visits that our boys found the water inviting, and the older set dipped in for a quick swim. All in all, this hike is a short but delightful trip to a gem of a spot.

Fun diversions for kids are found early in the hike to Lukens Lake.

The short hike to Lukens Lake is forested much of the way.

 Tuolumne Grove of Giant Sequoias

Stroll along a trail through a grove of astounding trees, including some great chances to get up close and personal with a few of these giants.

Distance: 2.5 miles roundtrip
Elevation change: 400 feet
Time: 2 hours
Starting point: Embark on this trail from the large parking area at the farthest west end of Tioga Road, very close to its intersection with Big Oak Flat Road near the Crane Flat area.

Heading down the trail to the grove, your group may begin to wonder what the big deal is. As you continue through a forested area on the old Big Oak Flat Road, heading down, down, down, you may start trying to guess if each big tree you see might be

It's hard to convey how large these trees are.

Have you ever seen a tree so large that you can fit in a tunnel through its root ball?

a giant sequoia. They aren't. Believe us: you will know one for sure when you see it. And yes, it is worth it! Get those kids moving down the trail to the grove and get ready for a good time.

When you come to the turnoff from the mostly paved road you have been traveling, a sign indicates that the grove is to the right along a trail resembling a figure eight. It doesn't matter what route you take, but be sure to make it around the whole way. You can surprise your kids with trees they can walk in, through, under, and around. We guarantee they will find something to be amazed by. We like to keep a few features on these adventures as surprises for our kids. While you might think that telling kids about the experiences that lie ahead could motivate them to keep hiking, we find that it often backfires when we have built up expectations that might not measure up. Try surprising your kids with what they will find along the way.

Our final tip for this hike: save a good pile of snacks for the hike up! It is all uphill once the tree-hugging fun is done. We coaxed our five-year-old up the trail by baiting him with fish-shaped crackers. Dole them out slowly, making your kid chew and swallow each one before handing out another. By making sure everyone in your group is properly fueled, you can finish off the trip in good spirits.

 ## Clouds Rest

If you have capable older kids with a thirst for adventure, Clouds Rest could be your family's favorite hike in Yosemite—or ever! This long hike has some steep climbs and a lot of exposure at the end as the trail traverses a narrow ridge. But the thrill of that narrow trail and the expansive views in literally every direction made this hike our older boys' most memorable experience in Yosemite. We bet it will also impress you and your children.

Distance: 14.5 miles roundtrip
Elevation change: 1775 feet
Time: 7–10 hours
Starting point: The trailhead is on Tioga Road at the west end of Tenaya Lake. Look for signs for "Sunrise" because this trailhead is also used to access the Sunrise High Sierra Camp.

This challenging trail will take most of a day, so be realistic in your evaluation of your family's capabilities. If you are willing and able to do it, we can promise that you will remember this destination forever.

Immediately after leaving the parking lot, cross Tenaya Creek by hopping from stone to stone. Depending on water levels, you may get slightly wet. We each removed our hiking boots and socks in order to keep our feet dry—14 miles is a long way to go with wet feet, and you'd almost surely develop blisters. The trail is mostly rolling for the first couple of miles with another small creek crossing facilitated by fallen logs, but at mile 2 you start

Iconic views from Clouds Rest

to climb in earnest. This section of the trail is steep and rocky, with a lot of switchbacks. The climb over the next mile is pretty unrelenting, as you gain 1000 feet in elevation.

When you reach the first junction, stop for a breather and appreciate the fact that the hardest part of the trail is behind you. The left fork goes to the Sunrise High Sierra Camp, but take the right fork and descend into a beautiful little drainage with numerous wildflowers, such as lupine, Indian paintbrush, wild daisies, and columbine, along the trail. Appreciating alpine and subalpine wildflowers requires slowing down and often stooping down. The varieties hearty enough to grow at these elevations are usually compact and low to the ground. The relative absence of water and the sometimes harsh wind and weather mean they need to keep their foliage to a minimum and hug the ground. Each member of our family has felt wonder and amazement when taking the time to study these miniature masterpieces and appreciate what it takes to survive in the high country.

The trail from this point rolls up and down for another 2 miles, passing a beautiful lake along the way. The trail here is not flat, but it is pleasant and interesting. Eventually you come into more open terrain with plentiful granite and fewer trees, and as you reach the next fork, you meet the John Muir Trail, which goes left. Once again you stay to the right, and once again the trail starts to climb, but less dramatically than before.

Soon you come to the top of the ridge. Looking north and back to Tenaya Lake near where we had started, our kids were impressed to see how far they had come. From here the trail continues to climb up the spine of the ridge and you will see that this ridge is getting narrower and narrower. This trend continues until you are on a path that is no wider in places than the average car, with steep sides falling away on the right and left. Some people, both children and adults, find it scary, while others find it invigorating, but you would really have to blunder badly to fall far enough to either side to be in true danger.

This final, narrow approach is all the more remarkable for the incredible views surrounding you. You feel like you are on top of the world, with the stunning landscape of the Yosemite high-country wilderness stretching out before you in every direction. Eventually you reach the high point on the ridge, and the terrain flattens out to an area roughly 50 feet in diameter, where you can take a seat, enjoy a snack, and revel in the scenery around you as you take a million pictures. There before you, and 1000 feet *below* you, is majestic Half Dome. All of the Yosemite Valley is laid out before you like a massive gash in the earth's crust. It is truly rewarding to have such a commanding view of this inspiring region. Enjoy it.

From here, simply follow the trail back the way you came, encouraging other hikers who are still working their way up. You still have 7 miles to go to return to your car, but you'll take solace in knowing that it is basically all downhill from here.

Your kids won't soon forget the astonishing panorama from Clouds Rest.

Adventures beyond Hiking

Adding more adventure to your trip means more engagement and interest from your kids. Here we share more details on area-specific activities to help get your kids out of the car!

Bicycling

There are few safe opportunities for biking in this region. Bikes are allowed only on paved trails, which are mostly nonexistent. Of course, if you brought your own bikes and are camped in one of the NPS campgrounds, you can always let your children ride around the camp area.

Boating

While boat tours are not offered in Yosemite, feel free to bring your own personal nonmotorized craft if you like to get out on the water. Please be sure to follow regulations regarding cleaning boats before entering park waters to minimize the spread of invasive species.

With the exception of Tenaya Lake, most of the lakes and rivers in this area involve quite a bit of hiking to access either the put-in, the take-out, or both. Use one of the many access points along Tioga Road to paddle out onto Tenaya Lake and enjoy the scenery.

Rock Climbing

This region is loaded with great opportunities to get off-trail and personal with a large piece of granite. Whether you come with a lot of experience or are trying out climbing for the first time, there is a place for you here. The wonderful guides at the Yosemite Mountaineering and Guide Service offer you all the help you need. They rent gear to experienced climbers, guide climbers on new routes, and offer lessons to people of all ages and experience levels, with requirements for adult accompaniment below a certain age.

A day of driving along Tioga Road will give you a small taste of how many opportunities this region offers. Consider giving your kids a taste of adventure with a rock-climbing and rappelling lesson they won't soon forget! Reservations are recommended and classes take up to seven hours, so plan to devote most of a day to this activity if you decide to try it.

Fishing

Many of the lakes and streams in this region of the park have been stocked with trout, and it is always a good idea to check with the rangers to see which bodies of water might be holding the most fish. In our travels here, we have seen kids catching fish in Middle Gaylor Lake (the first lake you reach on that hike), and we also saw a lot of pan-sized trout in Snow Creek, which runs along the road that takes you to the May Lake parking area. In the lakes, casting lures is probably the easiest way to catch trout from the bank, as it allows you to get your lure out farther even if there is some wind. On the small streams fishing with flies can be very effective. If you and your kids aren't expert fly casters, you can just as easily tie a fly on your line behind a small bobber and make your casts that way.

Trout in mountain streams don't tend to be picky about the specific fly that is presented to them, but they are very skittish if they see you approaching the edge of the stream. Approach slowly, use the shadows to break up your outline, and stay back from the edge a few feet to go undetected. Fly patterns that imitate terrestrial insects like ants and beetles usually work well in the summer months, but really, the fish in these mountain streams are not usually picky. Any bushy, attractor pattern is likely to get the attention of the fish.

Swimming

While swimming is allowed in almost all water in Yosemite (May Lake being the main exception, as it is used for High Sierra Camp drinking water), it isn't recommended everywhere. The rivers of the park can be slow and meandering in one area but frothy and raging a short distance away. It is easy to get caught in a current unexpectedly and swept away. The water is also quite cold, especially here in the high country. Snowmelt water is clear and inviting, but it can take your breath away in a hurry. Be very careful when taking your kids into rivers in this area. Some spots around the park are certainly better than others, especially for the youngest kids. There is a decent wading area to the side of the bridge leading across Tuolumne Meadows toward Parsons Memorial Lodge. After you cross the bridge, look for a sandy area to your left where people often stop to dip their feet. Another great spot is along the hike to Lyell Canyon. Multiple places on the hike make for good foot soaking. Again, choose your spot wisely, taking into account worst-case scenarios.

The shallow west end of Tenaya Lake is great for wading.

As for lakes in this area, time on the east end of Tenaya Lake can't be beat. There is a fabulous sand and gravel beach there that attracts sunbathers and swimmers alike. If you prefer a private beach spot, you are more likely to find it among the boulders on the west end of the lake. The water here is shallow and wonderful for wading!

Services and Amenities

Tuolumne Meadows and points along Tioga Road are rather remote. Because the Inyo National Forest butts up against the western edge of the park, there are no services in the immediate area. The town of Lee Vining is about forty minutes away from the Tioga Pass Entrance station and has expensive gas, restaurant, and grocery options. The Mobil is an especially memorable store with a deli and plenty of snacks, as well as picnic tables; sometimes they even host live music.

One of several historical sites in the Wawona area

Inside the park you will find a camp store, water spigots, and park information. The gas pump and tank that were once here have been removed due to environmental concerns. The park's new concessionaire, Aramark, now charges a fee for shuttle service in this area.

WAWONA

Added to the park in 1932, more than forty years after its founding, the Wawona area has a different feel from the more rugged landscapes in the rest of the park. Here you will find luxurious Victorian architecture in the Big Trees Lodge, manicured lawns, white picket fences, and covered bridges. Many of the area's historical buildings were originally built elsewhere in the park and then moved here in the 1950s and 1960s when the park shifted more to a natural, wilderness aesthetic. Some of these historic buildings still function, such as the blacksmith shop. Some easy trails in this area lead to smaller waterfalls and expansive

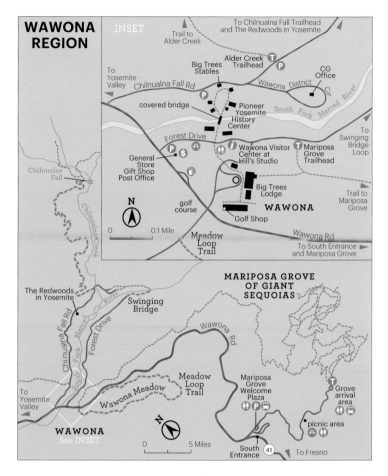

meadows that are great for younger kids. Featuring modest hikes with fewer crowds, Wawona is about a forty-five-minute drive from Yosemite Valley.

Things You Need to Know

If you are looking to provide your children with a taste of the western cowboy experience, this is the only area of the park that offers horseback rides. The Pioneer Yosemite History Center even offers stagecoach rides. The center includes a number of historical buildings from around the park, some of which are open for demonstrations. Wawona also has a golf course, which was grandfathered in when this area was added to the park in later years, a testament to the more developed feel of this section of the park.

In keeping with this region's celebration of Yosemite history, the visitor center is located in Hill's Studio, as a tribute to Thomas Hill, a painter from the 1800s. His work, along with that of other artists inspired by Yosemite, is featured in this small building. Rangers are on hand to answer questions, and the center sells books. There's a bathroom just off the porch out back.

Hiking Adventures

The Wawona area offers several pleasant hiking options that can be tailored to your family's abilities.

 Wawona Meadow Loop

An easy loop around a meadow, this trail is suitable for any ability level.

Distance: 3.5-mile loop around a large meadow
Elevation gain: Negligible
Time: 1.5–2.5 hours
Starting point: The trailhead is just across Wawona Road (State Route 41) from the Wawona Visitor Center and starts from the edge of the golf course.

This easy, flat loop (as the name implies) takes you around a very pretty meadow. In the morning and evening, you are likely to see deer and other wildlife in the meadow, and in the warmer parts of the day most of the route is shaded by trees that provide

The Wawona Meadow Loop offers shade and the chance to spot wildlife.

relief from the sun. In the spring and summer there are ample wildflowers in the meadow, and in the fall you are treated to gorgeous displays as the trees change color. Kids will particularly love the trickling streams that cross the trail. While one is small and seasonal, the other is larger and usually flows year round.

Be advised that this trail is frequented by horses from the riding stables found in this section of the park, and you know what type of gifts they leave behind on the trail. "Horse apples" have never really bothered us, as we met when we were working as wranglers on a dude ranch and shoveling plenty of it. We prefer to think of it as recycled grass fertilizer, but not everyone shares our perspective!

The new trail through the Mariposa Grove is inviting and accessible to kids of all ages.

Mariposa Grove of Giant Sequoias

This area features the largest group of sequoias in the park. They are so enormous that they hardly seem real!

Distance: 0.3 mile roundtrip for the Big Trees Loop, 2 miles for the Grizzly Giant Loop
Elevation gain: Negligible for the Big Trees Loop, 300 feet for the Grizzly Giant Loop
Time: 30 minutes–1.5 hours
Starting point: From the South Entrance, enter the roundabout and take the first righthand turn which takes you into the parking lot where the shuttle to the grove hiking area stops. If the lot is full, this turnoff will be gated shut. Your best bet is to try again later. In the meantime, continue on down the road about another 6 miles into the Wawona historical area to enjoy some of the activities there, hang out at the river, or hike another trail. Later head back down to the Mariposa Grove parking area and check to see if the gate is open.

If you are a guest at the Big Trees Lodge, you can use that facility's free shuttle. Simply ask for a ticket at the front desk.

The trail departs up and to the right of the main shuttle drop-off area. This is a good spot to fill up your water bottles and use the restroom before hiking. The Big Trees Trail is a short, wide, packed-gravel loop that circles a large meadow and includes the "Fallen Giant," an enormous fallen sequoia that lies alongside the trail. Railings keep you on the path and protect the meadow-habitat area, and interpretive signs share facts about these amazing giants of the forest.

The Grizzly Giant Trail branches off at the top of the first loop. If you are interested in seeing more astonishingly large trees, head up this trail to the right. The railing system mostly ends, and you begin to feel more like you are in a forest. The trail also heads slightly uphill until you reach the top of the loop, but with

Living giant sequoias aren't the only attraction in the Mariposa Grove.

benches and rest stops, and many huge trees to admire, you and your children will fare fine.

At the top of the loop the trail bends left and features a straight-on view of the Grizzly Giant. View the tree first from far away and then approach it until you are standing at its base, staring straight up into its towering height—an inspiring experience, one of our favorites in this area.

From this point, continue to the California Tunnel Tree, where you can walk straight into the depths of a fallen sequoia. Your kids will love the chance to finally get up close and personal with one of these giants. With the tree lying on the ground, you will all gain a new understanding of how large they really are!

After admiring the California Tunnel Tree, head back toward the shuttle area. We recommend turning around at the Grizzly

Giant. Even though you saw these sights on the way up, the downhill perspective is more interesting than the continuation of the loop. Plus, it cuts your round-trip distance a bit.

A brief note on pine cones: Along the trail you are bound to see some startlingly large pine cones. Which tree do you think they came from? The obvious answer is the giant sequoia. After all, it only makes sense that a tree that large would have huge pine cones, right? Good guess, but it turns out the opposite is true. The sugar pine makes these huge cones, while the sequoia's cones range from smaller than a dime to almost as big as a quarter. Your kids will likely be amazed by this seemingly contradictory fact!

Can you guess which cone comes from the giant sequoia? It might not be the one you think . . .

 Swinging Bridge

This short hike features a true swinging bridge over the South Fork of the Merced River.

Distance: 0.75 mile roundtrip
Time: Less than 1 hour
Starting point: From the Wawona General Store, drive 2 miles on Forest Drive to the fork in the road. The right fork enters the church camp parking area and the left goes to the trailhead parking area.

The swinging bridge over the South Fork of the Merced River is a fun spot to throw rocks and get little toes wet.

A clarification: two "swinging bridges" cross the Merced River. The one in Yosemite Valley is famous for the photographs taken upstream to Yosemite Falls—this is not that bridge. This true swinging bridge crosses the South Fork of the Merced River.

Straightforward up to the bridge, the trail forks into three paths after you cross it. Two paths require bushwhacking and then disappear, while the leftmost path takes you on a 4-mile loop through neighborhoods and on paved roads. For families, we recommend just the quick and easy jaunt to the bridge. Float some leaf-boats, toss a few rocks, and return the way you came.

Chilnualna Falls Trail

This strenuous climb leads to a series of five cascades. If your children are younger or you want easier hikes, we recommend instead spending time in the creek at the base of the trail.

Distance: 8.4 miles roundtrip
Elevation gain: 2300 feet
Time: 4–6 hours
Starting point: Just north of the Pioneer Yosemite History Center, find the Chilnualna Falls Road. Turn here and continue toward the parking lot near the end of this road, just over 1.5 miles down and through a private town (The Redwoods in Yosemite), complete with a school, post office, and library! Look for the dirt parking area on your right, just after the first bridge. From there, walk back onto the road and continue about one hundred yards to the trailhead.

Not up for a steep climb to Chilnualna Falls? Then hang out at the creek near the trailhead instead.

Near the beginning, at the first fork, a trail designated for horse traffic heads steeply uphill to the left. As you pass the horse fork, you reach the top of a rise. Look down to the right to see an enchanting creek and a bridge where the road continues over the water. When the trail forks again, stick to the leftmost path, the one designated for hikers.

Hiking to the uppermost falls is a challenge, as the trail climbs continuously. It is best for older children who really enjoy hitting the trail. However, if you are looking for a wonderful spot to enjoy cool creek water and shade, put this spot on your list. Kids can easily spend the entire morning or afternoon playing in the pools and on the boulders here. Scramble upstream or downstream across boulders if it's crowded, and you will find your own personal paradise.

Adventures beyond Hiking

The Wawona area offers fun activities beyond hiking for families. Choose to go on a horseback ride, line up a wagon tour, or enjoy the area's historical buildings.

Horseback Rides

The Wawona area is home to the lone riding stable in the park. Big Trees Stables offers two-hour rides around the Wawona Meadow Loop, an outing suitable for any level of experience. Riders must be at least 7 years old and 44 inches tall and cannot weigh more than 225 pounds. There are two tours in the morning and one in the early afternoon. See Resources for more information and to make reservations.

Wagon Tours

The Pioneer Yosemite History Center offers horse-drawn wagon rides on certain days for a small per-person fee. It is a relatively quick ride of fifteen to twenty minutes, but the driver shares a lot of interesting facts about the area that enhance the experience. It was difficult to find information online about the ride

Your kids might love a change of pace. How about a ride from Big Trees Stables?

schedule; check in at the visitor center when you first arrive so you can work the ride into your itinerary. At the time of this writing, rides were offered only in summer on Wednesday afternoons and from 10 a.m. to 2 p.m. Thursday through Sunday.

Park near the Wawona store, just downhill from the visitor center and Big Trees Lodge. If you are already in the parking area for those buildings, go out the back end of the lot and loop around and down to the store and history center parking, or go back out onto the main road and take the very next right into the same parking area.

From the parking area, you will see an old carriage barn full of antique wagons and carriages. You will also see the stables where the teams of horses are kept. Between these two buildings, slightly out of sight of the parking area, a covered bridge crosses the South Fork of the Merced River. Head onto the bridge, staying to the left to reserve the center for the horses. As you come out on the other side, look for the building ahead

The short but sweet wagon ride is sure to be a hit with kids.

and to the right with diamond-shaped windowpanes. This is the "stage coach" building where you can purchase your tickets to ride. The wagon seats about seven people comfortably.

If you aren't heading out on your ride immediately, walk around the historic center to check out the old buildings and read about their purposes. If the blacksmith shop is open, you can witness living history, which will engage your kids more fully. You may also want to enjoy some peaceful time in and around the water. Keep in mind that it may be better for you to cross the bridge back to the parking-lot side and find a path down to the river from there.

When it is time for your ride, meet the wagoner and his team in the shade on the history-center side of the covered bridge. Show him your tickets (but hang on to them for souvenirs), and he will tell you where to sit. The ride is about 10 minutes long—perfect for kids who might find the slow, dusty pace boring if it were much longer. Your knowledgeable, friendly wagoner will narrate the trip, but it is hard to hear if you aren't sitting in the front seat. You will get to ride around the history center, across the bridge, along the creek and then back again. The ride was bumpy, dusty, loud and wonderful—we can't recommend it enough!

Services and Amenities

The Wawona area offers a visitor center, a wilderness permit station, a grocery store, a gas station, and a lodge with dining.

YOUR FIRST YOSEMITE BACKPACKING TRIP

Getting even a mile off the beaten track will give you and your family a taste of what Yosemite represented to the early men and women explorers of this area. You will hike away from the crowds and into a part of California that you may never have known existed. The thought of putting everything on your back that you and your kids need for a couple of nights of sleeping outside may seem daunting, but the challenge is so worth it. If you honestly evaluate your skills and the abilities of the weakest, most vulnerable member of your family, and then decide you are up for it, you will experience awesome rewards.

Beyond the usual gear and preparation for any backpacking trip, this area requires special attention to food storage. Backpackers must store their food in a park-approved bear canister. They're available for rent at all the wilderness centers—you don't need to purchase one if you're an occasional backpacker.

Backpacking in Yosemite can be daunting, what with the presence of bears, the variable weather, the need to filter water, and the process involved in choosing a site and securing a permit. But if you follow certain precautions (see the Bears section in the Best Bets chapter), do your homework, choose your routes wisely, and plan your trip far enough in advance, all of those concerns can be easily addressed.

WILDERNESS PERMITS

Yosemite takes a different approach to backpacking than most other national parks. Instead of having specific campsites that

Opposite: Reflections on Elizabeth Lake

can be reserved, they put a limit on the number of backpackers who can enter a trailhead each day. Then, those backpackers who have secured a permit have the option of camping anywhere along the trail that they like, provided they travel beyond a certain minimum distance, which varies by trailhead. There are still some requirements for where you can camp, which take into account proximity to bodies of water and roads. Also, in the most popular areas and in places close to the High Sierra Camps, backpackers must stay in designated backcountry campgrounds, otherwise the large number of people dispersed around the area would harm the sensitive environment and result in a tent in every direction you looked. For more information on the High Sierra Camps, see the next section.

Of the daily quota for each trailhead, 60 percent can be reserved ahead of time for a small fee per person, and the other 40 percent are available on a first-come, first-served basis starting at 11:00 a.m. the day before your hike begins. The more popular trailheads fill up very quickly, but some trailheads nearly always have space available on any given day. Reservations can be made up to twenty-four weeks in advance, and first-come, first-served permits can be secured at any of six wilderness permit stations located in each of the main regions of the park. For more details, visit the park's website, and consult the sites suggested in the Resources section.

To help you prepare for your backpacking trip, the park service offers what it refers to as "backpackers camps," available to all wilderness permit holders, with the exception of those hiking Half Dome. For a nominal fee, park at the nearby trailhead and walk back to the campground, where you can spend the night before or after your permitted trip. Reservations are not necessary. The backpacker camp for Yosemite Valley is found behind North Pines Campground, across the footbridge. In Tuolumne Meadows the campsites are in the main campground, behind Loop A. The White Wolf area has sites at the back of the White Wolf Campground. Hikers

Stunning May Lake has the shortest approach distance of all the High Sierra Camps.

planning an overnight trip in the Wawona or Glacier Point areas may use the Yosemite Valley sites.

HIGH SIERRA CAMPS

Yosemite offers a unique way to experience the backcountry through its High Sierra Camps. Depending on which options you choose, these five camps offer either a small cabin or a canvas wall tent, and the staff prepares your breakfast and dinner for you. For an additional fee, they can even send you down the trail with a sack lunch for the day. They also provide mattresses, pillows, and blankets, leaving hikers to carry only a set of sheets or a sleep sack, plus their own personal items, such as clothing and toiletries. With this option you can hike the backcountry for multiple days with just a daypack, forgoing the heavier items that usually make up the bulk of a backpacker's gear. While not inexpensive, this option removes most of the biggest challenges associated with backpacking, and it can make for a great introduction to backpacking through the wilderness.

The High Sierra Camps form a loop throughout Tuolumne Meadows, with each camp spaced between 6 and 10 miles apart. Carrying only a daypack, most anyone can manage this distance over a full day, but if some members of your family cannot, you also have the option of renting mules to haul you to each camp. Because these camps are very popular, Aramark, the concessionaire, manages them via a lottery system. It pays to plan ahead if you're interested in this option. Learn more in the Resources section.

 May Lake

This short hike leads to an excellent camping destination. As this is the site of a High Sierra Camp, you have the option of paying for their services or carrying your own gear and setting up your tent in the designated campground. Dispersed camping is prohibited due to the high volume of campers.

Distance: 1.2 miles
Elevation gain: Moderate in one section
Time: 1–2 hours to camp
Starting point: Begin from the May Lake parking area, at the end of the spur road just west of Olmstead Point and Tenaya Lake on Tioga Road.

This designated campground shares a location with the May Lake High Sierra Camp. The campground is located a short walk from the shores of this beautiful lake, with massive granite formations to gaze at or explore on the far side of the lake. For more details, refer to the hiking description for this trail (see Tuolumne Meadows in the Yosemite Adventures by Region chapter). This is the shortest option for a backpacking excursion, and the destination will not disappoint.

Glen Aulin

While it's on the longer side, this backpacking option involves minimal elevation gain. You'll get to soak up stunning views of the surrounding peaks, climb on granite slabs, and linger along the Tuolumne River. You can either pay for the concessionaire's service at the High Sierra Camp or bring your own equipment and stay in the designated campground area.

Distance: 6 miles one way

Elevation gain: Minimal

Time: 2–3 hours each way if you keep at it, but you'll want to stop and appreciate the sights along the way

Starting point: The trailhead for this camp is adjacent to the riding stables at the Lembert Dome parking and picnic area in Tuolumne Meadows.

From the trailhead, it is less than 0.1 mile to Soda Springs and Parsons Memorial Lodge, which are definitely worth a stop (described in more detail in the Tuolumne Meadows portion of the Yosemite Adventures by Region chapter). From here the trail is mostly flat to downhill for about the next 4 miles, and then loses most of its elevation in the last mile before camp. This last part is also quite stunning as the Tuolumne River picks up speed and tumbles over granite. The flat trail and surrounding views will make the miles slip past quickly.

The campsite is right next to the White Cascade waterfall and just a short distance from Tuolumne Falls, which you pass on your way in. From camp, you can walk a short way downstream to view three more waterfalls.

 Cathedral Lakes

This trail's payoff includes some of the park's prettiest alpine lakes.

Peace and serenity are benefits of backpacking to a campsite.

Distance: 3.5 miles one way
Elevation Gain: 1000 feet
Time: 2.5–3.5 hours
Starting point: The Cathedral Lakes Trailhead is located a short distance west of the Tuolumne Meadows Visitor Center on Tioga Road.

At the lower of the two lakes, dispersed camping is prohibited because of the area's popularity. The 3.5 miles from Tuolumne Meadows are part of the John Muir Trail, and over this distance you gain 1000 feet in a noticeable but not too challenging climb. From the west end of the lower lake, you can gaze down on Tenaya Lake less than a mile away. Another bonus feature is the camp's proximity to the upper lake and the trail beyond. This region is filled with gorgeous meadows surrounded by iconic granite peaks such as Echo, Tresidder, and the Columbia Finger. This area is popular for a reason.

YOSEMITE CAMPING AND LODGING

Yosemite National Park encompasses a large area, so it helps to be strategic about your camping or lodging choices. If you end up sleeping far away from your day's activities, you may be surprised at how much time you will spend in the car. For that reason, we have broken up the accommodations into four regions: the Yosemite Valley, North of the Valley, Glacier Point and Wawona, and Tuolumne (which includes the campgrounds along the higher portions of Tioga Road). All of the campgrounds in the lower elevations are within a forty-minute drive of the Valley, but if you find yourself camping up high near Tuolumne yet spending the day in the Valley and Glacier Point, plan on a lot of windshield time.

Another challenge of camping in Yosemite is securing reservations. While this process is handled online and reservations go on sale four to five months ahead of time, the more popular sites and weekends sell out within minutes (see Resources). We provide some helpful tips for reserving a site, but if you don't secure a reservation or are planning a trip on shorter notice, we also have strategies for the first-come, first-served sites.

You may also want to consider nearby national forest campgrounds. Although they're outside the park boundaries, they can serve as a great backup option when it's hard to get a campsite in the park.

East of the park, between Lee Vining and the Tioga Pass entrance station along State Route 120 there are four campgrounds, with an additional two just off the highway. Part of the Inyo National Forest, they are all first-come, first-served. Even on a busy weekend in late July we were able to acquire a site

YOSEMITE CAMPING AND LODGING OPTIONS

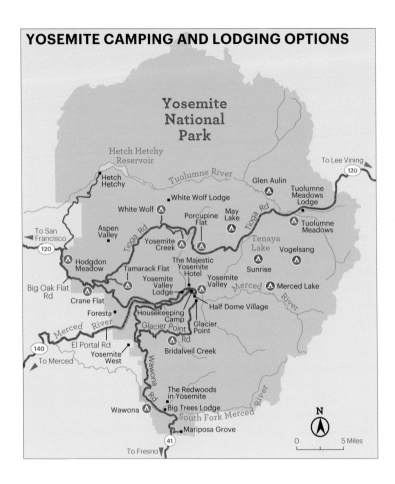

with little difficulty. If you aren't having any luck finding an open spot, talk to the camp host (who is often spread across multiple campgrounds, so you might have to hunt him down or wait at his trailer). The host usually knows who might be leaving soon or will be able to find you a spot near his site. We found these sites very pleasant with a relaxed atmosphere, and we were still very close to park activities.

QUICK TIPS FOR RESERVING CAMPGROUNDS

When we plan our trips to the parks, we always like to have a spot reserved at a camp or lodge for the first night's stay. That way when we are driving to our destination we don't feel rushed and stressed, worrying about whether we will have a place to sleep that night. Later, based on our preferred activities, we strategically target a campground closer to that day's events. If we can secure a reservation there, great. If not, we know that we have to get up early and drive first to the new campground to snag one of those first-come, first-served spots. There isn't a great mystery behind how to get one of the latter—the early bird gets the worm.

To get an earlier start, we will often plan to eat a cold breakfast like cereal or bagels that morning so we can break camp faster. Or we may even pack a breakfast like muffins and fruit the kids can eat in the car on the way. Another tip is to drive through the campground scouting for people who look like they are packing up to leave. Once you locate a potential spot, politely ask if they are departing that day. If so, you can usually leave an item like a camp chair in their spot to hold it while you go fill out the paperwork for the site and then leave the appropriate tag on the site marker. You can then head off for the day knowing you will have a spot to return to that evening.

On the western side of the park you pass through the Stanislaus National Forest. While there are fewer campgrounds available in this area, the closest one is the Dimond O Campground, with thirty-eight sites that you can reserve by phone or online (see Resources).

LODGING

Whether you are simply not the camping type or are maybe a bit concerned about bears or weather in this particular park, do not

Yosemite National Park Campgrounds

CAMPGROUND	NUMBER OF SITES	DATES OPEN (depending on weather)	RESERVATIONS AVAILABLE
Yosemite Valley			
Upper Pines	238	Year-round	Yes
Lower Pines	60	March 30–Nov. 30	Yes
North Pines	81	March 26–Nov. 5	Yes
Camp 4	35	Year-round	No
North of the Valley			
Hodgdon Meadow	105	Year-round	Yes
Crane Flat	166	May 27–Oct. 15	Yes
Tamarack Flat	52	May 24–Oct. 15	No
South of the Valley			
Bridalveil Creek	110	July 1–Sept. 17	No
Wawona	93	Year-round	Yes
Tuolumne Region			
White Wolf	74	June 15–Oct. 1	No
Yosemite Creek	75	July 1–Sept. 4	No
Porcupine Flat	52	July 6–Oct. 15	No
Tuolumne Meadows	304	June 15–Sept. 24	Yes, for half (50%) of sites

Source: NPS website.

worry! In the indoor (and quasi-indoor) sleeping arrangement category, you can choose from many excellent options. The summaries that follow will assist you in choosing the one that suits your family best. When you find something that sounds interesting, visit www.travelyosemite.com for more information.

TOILET	WATER	RVS (in feet)	TRAILER (in feet)	COST (US dollars in 2018)
Flush	Tap	35	24	$26
Flush	Tap	40	35	$26
Flush	Tap	40	35	$26
Flush	Tap	No	No	$6 per person
Flush	Tap	40	30	$26
Flush	Tap	40	30	$26
Vault	Creek (must purify)	Not recommended	Not recommended	$12
Flush	Tap	35	24	$18
Flush	Tap	35	35	$26
Flush	Tap	27	24	$18
Vault	Creek (must purify)	Not recommended	Not recommended	$12
Vault	Creek (must purify)	Not recommended	Not recommended	$12
Flush	Tap	35	35	$26

YOSEMITE VALLEY

The Valley offers a wide range of camping and lodging choices, nestled on the Valley floor with quick access to all the hiking and adventures found in this region. They are the best option if you plan to visit the Valley, but they fill up fast.

Bear boxes, picnic tables, and fire rings typical of Yosemite campgrounds

Camping

This region has four campgrounds: Upper Pines, Lower Pines, North Pines, and Camp 4. Reservations are accepted for all three Pines campgrounds, but Camp 4 is first-come, first-served. Make reservations for the other three at www.recreation.gov.

Upper, Lower, and North Pines: These campgrounds are all adjacent to one another at the far eastern end of Yosemite Valley, along the shores of the Merced River. Upper Pines is the largest and farthest east with 238 sites, while Lower Pines has just 60 sites. On the far side of the Merced River, North Pines, with 81 sites, is bordered on the other side by Tenaya Creek.

Each site has a fire ring, bear box, and picnic table and is near bathrooms with drinking water and flush toilets. You are not permitted to wash dishes at your site, so you will probably want to bring a plastic bin, crate, or other container to carry your dishes and washing implements to and from the wash area. Also come prepared to haul water for drinking. A collapsible wagon or small cart is ideal.

Camp 4: This camp has just 35 sites that are for tents only, and you have to walk a short distance to reach them. Open year-round, it is the only camp that forbids pets.

Old-world charm and great service greet you at The Majestic Yosemite Hotel.

Lodging

Yosemite Valley offers the widest range of lodging options, from luxurious hotels to more basic "glamping" options where you have more structure around you than a nylon or canvas tent, but you are still out in the open air. All lodges are booked through the website www.travelyosemite.com, where you can find more details, photos, and maps for each location.

The Majestic Yosemite Hotel

Classified as a AAA Four Diamond hotel, The Majestic Yosemite Hotel (formerly the Awhahnee Hotel) represents the ultimate in luxury and service. It offers several levels of rooms with various views of the surrounding Valley, as well as several types of cottages. It has a fabulous dining room, a cozy sitting room, and outdoor porches with views across the Valley. This hotel has it all.

Yosemite Valley Lodge

If you are looking for a recently remodeled and beautiful hotel, the Yosemite Valley Lodge will meet your needs in a more moderate price range. Because they are less expensive, these rooms sell out quickly. Book them far in advance.

Canvas wall tents in Half Dome Village (Photo by Miquel Vieira, Creative Commons)

Half Dome Village

A more rustic option, Half Dome Village (formerly Curry Village) comprises a mix of cabins and canvas wall tents that keep visitors comfortable while providing a more outdoorsy experience. Your children can stay in hotel rooms most anywhere, but how often do they get to stay in a canvas wall tent like the pioneers did? Have realistic expectations, however. Calling a sheet of canvas a "wall" does not mean that it will have the same sound-blocking features of a true wall, so you'll be aware of what's happening next door. Consider earplugs for light sleepers if you opt to stay in this area.

Housekeeping Camp

Nestled along the shores of the Merced River, this camp epitomizes the idea of "glamping." The units have walls on three sides, but a canvas roof above that also covers an adjacent patio with a picnic table for meals. Inside are a table and chairs, bunk beds, and a double bed—room to sleep six. Typically, guests bring their own sleeping bags or bedding to throw down on the mattresses, but bedding can also be rented as needed.

The accommodations at Housekeeping Camp (Photo by advencap, Creative Commons)

NORTH OF THE VALLEY

Hodgdon Meadow Campground (105 sites) is located just inside the Big Oak Flat Entrance, making it a good option for your first night if you are coming into the park from that direction. Its campsites are in a mostly forested setting.

Crane Flat Campground (166 sites) is near the junction of Big Oak Flat and Tioga Roads, a thirty-minute drive from the Valley. The tent sites in this campground are also mostly forested, but they look out onto a series of small meadows that attract some wildlife.

Technically located on Tioga Road, Tamarack Flat Campground (52 sites) is so close to the junction with Big Oak Flat Road that we felt it belonged in this region. At the junction of two streams that divide the camp into several areas, it has on average a bit more spacing between sites for added privacy. Your only option for drinking water is the creek. Be prepared to boil or purify by another method, or bring enough for all your cooking and drinking needs.

PRIVATE LODGING IN OR ACCESSED THROUGH THE PARK

Four private areas are accessed through or located in the park: the town of Yosemite West and the inholdings of Foresta, The Redwoods in Yosemite, and Aspen Valley. They are not owned or operated by the NPS but could be good back-up options for lodging.

A small grouping of resort homes, Yosemite West is located off Wawona Road on the west side of the park just south of the Arch Rock Entrance. Accommodations here are about thirty minutes from Yosemite Valley and Wawona and only 7 miles from the ski and snowboard park with Glacier Point just beyond. If you are interested in the many lodging options, hotels, and private vacation homes in this area, try searching online for "West Yosemite."

Foresta is one of three private enclaves within the park boundaries. Properties here were owned before the park was founded and thus exist as private inholdings. Situated off Big Oak Flat Road, a handy location for Valley access, Foresta does not have any commercial properties, but many of its homes are operated as vacation rentals. Search online for more details about specific rentals if this community is of interest.

In the Wawona area, the Redwoods in Yosemite is another private community within the borders of the park. An ideal spot from which to explore the history-rich southern end of the park, it does not have commercial accommodations like hotels, but you might explore some vacation home options in the area, ranging from log cabins to spacious homes.

The final private option, Aspen Valley in the Tuolumne Meadows area, is a bit more difficult to research. Instead of looking for details via a general internet search, try searching directly on a vacation rental site like www.vrbo.com or www.airbnb.com.

Tents and RVs scattered among the trees at Wawona Campground

GLACIER POINT AND WAWONA

We group the Glacier Point and Wawona camping and lodging together since they are both south of the Valley. Glacier Point is about equidistant between the Valley and Wawona, so if you can't find a place to stay in Wawona, Glacier Point is the next closest in-park choice.

Camping

Along Glacier Point Road, Bridalveil Creek Campground (110 sites) is about a forty-five-minute drive from both the Yosemite Valley and the Wawona area. It is quite high at an elevation of 7200 feet, mostly forested, and bordered on two sides by small creeks with another running through the campground that can be fun for kids to splash in on hot days.

Wawona (93 sites) is the park's southernmost campground. It is a few miles north of all the activities of the Pioneer Yosemite History Center and the Mariposa Grove of Giant Sequoias. Its three loops are near the South Fork of the Merced River, which during the summer is small enough to provide some good play spots. Loops B and especially C are a bit farther from Wawona Road.

Lodging

This section of the park features Big Trees Lodge, located close to the Wawona Visitor Center. This area has a different feel than the rest of the park due to the Victorian architecture of the stately lodge, manicured lawns, nine-hole golf course, riding stables, and historical buildings. The lodge also boasts an outdoor pool. The rooms consist of 54 standard hotel-style rooms with a shared bath and 50 with private baths, all scattered among six whitewashed historic buildings. In the evening, enjoy music in the lounge or soak in the surroundings from one of the extensive verandas. For more information on all lodging options, visit www.travelyosemite.com.

TUOLUMNE REGION

Here we highlight not only the options strictly in Tuolumne Meadows but also those along Tioga Road. Keep in mind that if you can't find a place to stay in the park, there are many Forest Service campgrounds just outside this northeastern entrance.

Camping

The westernmost campground in the high-country region of Tioga Road, White Wolf Campground (74 sites) is nestled between two small seasonal creeks that may or may not have water during your stay. This campground is more wooded and private than those lower down and features large granite boulders for kids to climb.

Yosemite Creek Campground (75 sites) offers tent sites on the shores of several small creeks that intersect within the immediate area and are great for playing in. Its twisty roads mean that RVs and trailers are not recommended, making it more private than many of the larger campgrounds. It is close to all the upper regions of Yosemite.

Victorian style Big Trees Lodge

Smaller and more secluded than many of the other campgrounds in Yosemite, and close to a lot of the great sights and hikes of the high country, Porcupine Flat Campground (52 sites) is roughly divided in two by Porcupine Creek. Its eastern loop has some large granite boulders that can be fun for kids to play on and is also a bit farther from Tioga Road. Your only options for drinking water at Yosemite Creek and Porcupine Flat are the creeks that flow through the campgrounds. Be prepared to boil or purify water, or bring enough for cooking and drinking.

The largest option in the high country, Tuolumne Meadows Campground (304 sites) is located close to the visitor center, post office, camp store, and other services. Less secluded than other campgrounds in this region, it is very convenient to services and this region's features and amenities. The campground sits on a large, flat, treed bench just across the road from its namesake. Campers can take in many inspiring views and are likely to glimpse herds of deer feeding in the meadows.

Mule deer in Tuolumne Meadows in the late afternoon

Lodging
This region features two lodges and the High Sierra Camps.

Tuolumne Meadows Lodge
This lodge sits in the high country at 8700 feet, so it is open for a relatively short time from mid-June to September, weather permitting. Close to some of the best hiking options in Yosemite, it comprises 69 canvas wall tents located in an alpine meadow with a stream.

White Wolf Lodge
Situated in a mountain meadow ringed with trees, White Wolf Lodge offers a degree of solitude with just 24 canvas wall tents and

4 cabins. Guests eat in a central dining room located in a common building with a nice porch for enjoying your surroundings.

High Sierra Camps
The Tuolumne area is home to the High Sierra Camps, which offer lodging that you have to hike to. To learn more about them, refer to the Your First Yosemite Backpacking Trip chapter.

SAFETY IN THE PARK

Parents should take precautions to keep their family safe on their Yosemite National Park adventure. Prepare for the conditions you could encounter and bring supplies to help with any mishaps. The elevation in this park, in particular, may challenge some visitors, especially people who live at sea level, although these effects *can* be mitigated somewhat in some cases by your physical fitness.

WEATHER AND HOW TO PREPARE FOR IT

The chart below shows the average temperatures and days of precipitation per month in the Yosemite Valley, which is at an altitude of roughly 4000 feet. Along Tioga Road near Tuolumne Meadows, the elevations are closer to 8000 feet, and you can expect the temperatures to be cooler by 10 to 20 degrees Fahrenheit. As you can see, the temperature swings from early morning to midafternoon in these mountain settings can be quite

Weather Averages for Yosemite National Park					
	JANUARY	**FEBRUARY**	**MARCH**	**APRIL**	**MAY**
Yosemite Valley					
High Temperature	48	53	58	65	73
Low Temperature	28	30	33	37	43
Days of Precipitation	8	7	9	6	3
Tuolumne Meadow					
High Temperature	43	41	46	48	55
Low Temperature	9	8	12	16	24
Days of Precipitation	11	10	11	7	5

Source: NPS website.

dramatic, so you need to plan a strategy for keeping everyone comfortable. Come prepared for every possible kind of weather; dress in layers and bring adequate raingear. Outfitting an entire family with good gear can get expensive, but you don't need to go overboard with everyone dressed in top-of-the-line apparel suitable for an Everest expedition.

An inexpensive fleece jacket provides excellent insulation— just avoid anything made of cotton or cotton-blends, including hoodies and other sweatshirts. These may be fine for sweating in the gym, but when cotton gets wet, it loses almost all of its insulation value. By contrast, clothing made of synthetic fiber or wool maintains its insulation value when wet from the sweat of exertion or an afternoon thunderstorm.

Breathable, waterproof fabrics are the most effective, although they come at a price, and lightweight versions can be quite expensive. These technical fabrics are especially important for long-distance backpackers, but for shorter adventures, a simple nonbreathable waterproof shell or a rain poncho costs a lot less and will still keep you dry during an unexpected rain shower even if you get a bit clammy while wearing it. Reliable gear increases your family's enjoyment, comfort, and safety while hiking, but you don't need to break the bank or be dissuaded

JUNE	JULY	AUGUST	SEPTEMBER	OCTOBER	NOVEMBER	DECEMBER
82	90	90	84	72	57	47
50	56	55	50	41	32	27
1	1	0	2	3	5	7
64	72	71	66	57	47	41
30	37	35	30	24	16	9
3	3	3	3	5	9	10

from participating in the outdoors because you can't afford all the latest trends in backcountry gear.

A couple of relatively inexpensive but necessary specialty items include a warm hat and wool or synthetic socks. Hats are lightweight, easy to carry (take one, take two!), and go a long way toward keeping kids warm in a pinch, because we humans lose a lot of heat through our head and ears. On hot days, a hat with a brim also aids in sun protection. Wool socks have come a long way the past couple decades; they are soft and comfortable these days. You can find deals online for merino wool socks, even in kids' sizes, and the finer gauge of this wool makes it nonitchy and even more effective as insulation. Wool also has natural odor-fighting properties (very handy!) and wicks away moisture, helping to prevent blisters—a definite plus, especially for kids. We splurged on some for our family and the kids love them. They have made the many miles we have hiked much more pleasant. Cotton socks are *not* recommended because they are not warm when wet.

Lightning

Yosemite does not get a lot of rain, but when clouds gather, generally more likely in the late afternoon, there is always a risk of lightning strikes on the upper reaches of the park's massive granite formations. When you or the kids spot dark clouds forming on the horizon, you need to think about finding shelter soon. You can tell how far away you are from a storm by counting: the speed of sound is approximately 340 miles (1115 feet or 0.21 mile) per second, depending on temperature and elevation. So if you see a lightning flash and count five seconds until you hear thunder, you are *only 1 mile* away from the lightning. Don't wait to find out how close you are. Get down off the mountain as soon as you see the storm coming! Get off of high points and find a group of trees of moderate and equal height. Don't be the tallest thing out there, and don't stand under the tallest tree in the area in case it becomes a lightning rod.

Even a fallen giant sequoia is impressive.

Positive experiences in nature enhance a child's self-image. (Photo by Katie Grullón)

ELEVATION AND ALTITUDE SICKNESS

As you may remember from science class, the higher you go, the less dense the air is. At higher elevations (farther from sea level), air particles are more spread out, and a normal breath of air contains fewer air molecules and therefore less oxygen. If you live at lower elevations, you will probably notice that you are breathing a little harder when exerting yourself in the high country of Yosemite and your hiking pace may be slower.

Most people can handle the change of altitude up to 8000 feet with little problem. How will you know if you or your child isn't handling it well? Altitude sickness brings on a collection of flulike symptoms, including headache, nausea, fatigue, and dizziness. Symptoms typically start six to eight hours after you ascend to altitude and generally subside in one to two days. Exertion exacerbates the problem. Returning to a lower elevation is the quickest fix, and fortunately most of the camping and lodging areas in Yosemite are in the lower regions.

DEHYDRATION

Yosemite has the dual challenge of being high in elevation and having a fairly dry climate. Breathing dry air into moist lungs causes you to lose water faster upon exhaling. Symptoms people attribute to altitude sickness are related to dehydration as often as they are to altitude. Make it a point for everyone in the family to stay hydrated by drinking a lot more during your Yosemite visit—you'll all feel better for it. It's often difficult to get younger children to drink enough fluids. You may not normally give your kids juices or flavored drinks, but when adventuring outdoors at altitude, choose hydration over concerns about sugary drinks. Those little tubes of individually sized drink mixes work well. Kids can choose their favorite flavors and add a tube to their water bottles. We also allow our kids to have sports drinks while we are exerting ourselves in the outdoors.

BEAR SAFETY

Somewhere between 300 and 500 bears roam Yosemite National Park, but this fact is not a cause for alarm. For starters, despite its prominent place on the state flag of California, grizzly bears have been extinct in the state since the 1920s. Rest assured that any bear you encounter will be the less formidable black bear. Males average about 250 pounds, whereas the females typically weigh in at around 150 pounds. Also, don't be confused by the name or your experience from elsewhere. Many black bears in the west, and most in Yosemite, are brown to blond in color, unlike the creatures farther east in the United States, which are usually black. But even if the bear is brown in color, in this part of the world it is still the black bear species.

In the entire history of the park, there has never been a fatality or even a serious injury from a bear. Statistically, you are unlikely to be the first of Yosemite's roughly four million annual visitors to get attacked by a bear.

However, we recommend that you do not become complacent because black bears can still cause a lot of damage to property and are especially intrigued by strong scents from food or toiletries, for instance. In the distant past, park rangers encouraged people-bear interactions with food and even had a few designated feeding stations for entertainment purposes, but this practice led to a lot of problems. The bears became more and more aggressive about getting to human food and would break car windows, rip open soft-sided campers, or even tear through back seats of cars to get into the trunk. These days, there are very strict rules for bear management within the park.

Bears have an amazing sense of smell and a voracious appetite. If they get even a faint whiff of something enticing, even strongly scented items that may not be food, they will be determined to check it out. Check the park's website to make sure you are complying with the current rules, but start by reviewing these food storage regulations:

If you want to take close-up shots of wildlife, a telephoto lens is useful.

- You may store food and other scented items in your car during the day when you are in it, but when you leave it unattended, you must move all food and other scented items, such as baby wipes, granola bar wrappers, and so on, out of sight and roll up all the windows.

- Because bears are generally more active at night, park visitors must remove all food from the car and store it overnight in a bearproof container or storage locker, provided at most campsites and many trailheads. Storing your food in easy-to-move plastic totes makes this chore much less cumbersome. You can keep food in a hard-sided camper or trailer, provided you close all the windows and vents.

- If you are in any campground or lodging with canvas wall tents, you must store your food in one of the provided food lockers. Keep them latched at all times, and treat your trash just like food, because it still smells good to a bear.

- On the trail, keep all food within arm's reach and never leave it unattended, whether in a backpack or anyplace else.

These scenarios, together with food left outside in campgrounds, represent the majority of modern-day bear incidents. If you are out hiking in an undeveloped area and see a bear, park rules require that you stay at least fifty yards away—close enough to get great photos while not disturbing the bear. If a bear approaches you, or if you are in a developed area like a campground or parking lot, try to scare it away by making loud noises, shouting, and standing as a group with other people in the area to intimidate it. Bear spray is prohibited in Yosemite National Park, unlike in other national parks with grizzlies.

Park rangers are doing their best to allow bears to maintain their natural aversion to humans, rather than leading them to associate people with an easy meal. Bears that become too aggressive sometimes are relocated or even killed. Rangers patrol areas periodically to monitor bear activity and at times even shoot bears with nonlethal projectiles like paint balls, rubber bullets, or small bean bags to foster a negative association with humans. As long as you follow the rules, you should have no reason to fear the park's ursine inhabitants.

HANTAVIRUS

With the preponderance of bears roaming the woods in Yosemite, you may be surprised to learn that the greater risk to your health comes from a different mammal, one that weighs less than an ounce. The ubiquitous deer mouse, found throughout the United States, is a carrier of a pathogen called hantavirus that can be quite dangerous, even lethal, resulting in an illness known as hantavirus pulmonary syndrome. Symptoms typi-

DISCLAIMER

Yosemite is fundamentally a wild place. While that is one of its greatest attractions, it also carries with it certain risks. We have done our best to provide reasonable advice and guidance on how to have a fun, safe, adventurous family vacation in the park, but there is no way that we can write a book that is a substitute for the reader's sound judgment. Conditions in the mountains change quickly, and only you can respond to those changes—a book cannot.

Every family has members with differing strengths and weaknesses. You know your family, and we do not. So do your research and make your plans, and then make the right decisions when you are in the park and faced with your specific circumstances. We are confident that with the right preparation and planning you will have a safe and excellent vacation, but we cannot *guarantee* that outcome.

cally present anywhere from one to eight weeks after exposure to an infected rodent's urine, saliva, blood, or droppings and are similar to those associated with the flu, such as a fever, fatigue, chills, and muscle aches. Some victims develop headaches, nausea, and vomiting. If you experience any of these symptoms after being exposed to rodents, seek medical help immediately.

The primary means of exposure is breathing in the virus. Use care to avoid stirring up dust in areas where rodents are likely nearby. Other precautions seem obvious, but people regularly ignore them—don't feed the rodents! We were surprised how often we saw park visitors handing out snacks to chipmunks, ground squirrels, etc. They inhabit many of the same places as mice. Finally, if you notice mouse activity or droppings in a room or canvas tent, alert the staff so that they can safely clean it up.

While statistically more common than serious bear injuries (of which there have been none in the park), cases of hantavirus are still extremely rare. There have only been three occurrences in the park's history, one in 2000 and another in 2010, neither of which were life threatening. In 2012, however, in an outbreak in some of the luxury tent cabins, ten people became sick, three of whom died. While this incident was tragic, with some basic precautions, you should feel free to enjoy all the park has to offer.

FIRST-AID KITS

Carrying a simple first-aid kit is always a good idea, but this precaution becomes especially important the farther you are from help. Having a first-aid kit in your car and on every hike and backpacking trip brings peace of mind and could save someone's life. Kits designed for your car are larger, heavier, and more fully stocked. Those built for hiking need to be small and light enough that you will actually bring them with you when you go. (When you're out on the trail, it isn't of much use to you if it's in the car or back at the campsite or hotel room.) All outdoor retailers and drugstores carry some type of first-aid kit. Find one that works for you and your family, and keep it handy.

You can easily create your own kit. Here are the basics we recommend. All of these supplies should easily fit in a quart-sized, sealable plastic bag:

☐ Tweezers. This simple tool is great for removing splinters or ticks; you may already have a pair on your pocketknife or multi-tool.

☐ Safety pins. They can secure bandage wraps and be used to create arm slings, etc. Get larger ones that are robust—old-fashioned baby diaper pins are the best.

☐ Bandanas. Use for splints and slings, or dip one in water to cool someone down who is overheating.

☐ Adhesive bandages of various sizes and shapes

☐ Medical tape and gauze bandages for larger wounds

☐ Antibiotic ointment

☐ Antiseptic wipes

- ☐ Moleskin for blisters. Duct tape works too, although it can leave a gooey residue on socks and skin.
- ☐ ACE bandage
- ☐ Acetaminophen, ibuprofen, or other medication (in age/weight-appropriate doses)
- ☐ Ibuprofen or naproxen sodium—helps prevent swelling and relieves pain.
- ☐ Antihistamine for allergic reactions
- ☐ Whatever other personal medications you or your kids require

TRAVEL CHECKLISTS

It never hurts to have a checklist—either for the fun of checking off the items or the security of knowing you didn't leave something important behind.

WILDLIFE CHECKLIST

Many more animals than this call the park home, but this list should keep your kids entertained and engaged. If you think you may have spotted a bird or animal not on this list that you cannot identify, ask a ranger or inquire about it at a visitor center.

Mammals

About 90 varieties of mammals live in Yosemite. Some of the most common include:

☐ Black bear (commonly brown in color in this region)
☐ Blacktail deer
☐ California ground squirrel
☐ Coyote
☐ Douglas squirrel
☐ Golden-mantled ground squirrel
☐ Yellow-bellied marmot
☐ Mule deer
☐ Pika
☐ Sierra Nevada bighorn sheep
☐ Western gray squirrel

Birds

More than 260 species of birds are known to live in Yosemite at some point during the year. Here are some to look for:

- ☐ Acorn woodpecker
- ☐ American robin
- ☐ Brown creeper
- ☐ California scrub jay (bright blue and gray with no crest)
- ☐ California towhee
- ☐ California valley quail
- ☐ Clark's nutcracker
- ☐ Common raven
- ☐ Dark-eyed junco
- ☐ European starling
- ☐ Golden-crowned kinglet
- ☐ Hermit thrush
- ☐ House sparrow
- ☐ Mountain chickadee
- ☐ Mountain quail
- ☐ Northern flicker
- ☐ Oak titmouse
- ☐ Sooty grouse
- ☐ Spotted towhee
- ☐ Steller's jay (dark blue with a black, crested top)
- ☐ Western scrub jay
- ☐ Wrentit
- ☐ Yellow-rumped warbler

Reptiles and Amphibians

Some of the most common include:

- ☐ Garter snake
- ☐ Pacific treefrog
- ☐ Sierra fence lizard
- ☐ Sierra mountain kingsnake
- ☐ Western pond turtle

FLORA CHECKLIST

Keep your eyes peeled for these trees and wildflowers:

Trees

- ☐ California black oak
- ☐ Douglas fir
- ☐ Giant sequoia
- ☐ Jeffrey pine
- ☐ Lodgepole pine
- ☐ Mountain hemlock
- ☐ Ponderosa pine
- ☐ Red fir
- ☐ Western juniper
- ☐ White fir

Wildflowers

- ☐ Columbine
- ☐ Lupine
- ☐ Monkeyflower
- ☐ Paintbrush
- ☐ Shooting stars
- ☐ Woolly mule's ears

DAY HIKING CHECKLIST

The Ten Essentials

The point of the Ten Essentials, originated by The Mountaineers, has always been to answer two basic questions: Can you prevent emergencies and respond positively should one occur (items 1–5)? And can you safely spend a night—or more—outside (items 6–10)? Use this list as a guide, and tailor it to the needs of your family.

1. Navigation: Map, compass, GPS
2. Headlamp or flashlight, spare batteries

3. Sun protection: Sunscreen, lip balm, sunglasses
4. First aid: See above list for kit contents; be sure to include moleskin/tape
5. Knife or multi-tool, duct tape, twine
6. Fire: Matches or lighter, waterproof container, fire starter
7. Shelter: Rain jackets at a minimum, could include a tarp or bivy sack
8. Extra food: Sugary and salty, especially for kids
9. Extra water: Water bottles or hydration system, water filter or treatment
10. Extra clothes: Jacket, vest, pants, gloves, hat

Other Useful Items

☐ Binoculars
☐ Camera
☐ Day pack
☐ Snacks, such as energy bars
☐ Insect repellent
☐ Toilet paper!

BACKPACKING CHECKLIST

This list is adapted from information on REI's website:
☐ The Ten Essentials (see list above)
☐ Backpack with rain cover
☐ Toilet paper and a trowel (bury human waste at least six inches deep and 200 feet from water sources; pack out toilet paper)
☐ Ground cloth for tent, if desired
☐ Sleeping bag
☐ Sleeping pad
☐ Pillow or stuffable sack
☐ Whistle and signaling mirror
☐ Meals
☐ Energy food and snacks, especially for kids!
☐ Stove
☐ Fuel

- ☐ Cookset with pot grabber
- ☐ Dishes, bowls, and/or cups
- ☐ Utensils
- ☐ Bear canister or rope to hang food on pole
- ☐ Backup water treatment system
- ☐ Spare clothing for number of days and a variety of weather conditions
- ☐ Backcountry permit
- ☐ Camera
- ☐ Binoculars
- ☐ Hand sanitizer and/or biodegradable soap
- ☐ Insect repellent
- ☐ Toothbrush and toothpaste
- ☐ Quick-dry towel

RESOURCES

PARK CONTACT INFORMATION

Yosemite National Park, Public Information Office,
PO Box 577, Yosemite, CA 95389

General questions: 209-372-0200 (then dial 3, then 5). Open
9:00 a.m. to 5:00 p.m. Pacific time (closed for lunch). If the system sends you back to the main menu, it means the ranger is on
the line with another caller—try again later.

HELPFUL ONLINE NPS RESOURCES

o Planning your visit: www.nps.gov/yose/planyourvisit/index
.htm
o Bear safety: www.nps.gov/yose/planyourvisit/bears.htm
o Lightning safety: www.nps.gov/yose/planyourvisit/lightning
.htm
o Backcountry reservations: www.nps.gov/yose/planyourvisit
/wildpermits.htm
o Maps: www.nps.gov/yose/planyourvisit/maps.htm. Order
maps and brochures: www.nps.gov/yose/contacts.htm
o Guide to the Mariposa Grove: www.nps.gov/yose/planyour-
visit/upload/mgrove.pdf
o Shuttle service: www.nps.gov/yose/planyourvisit/upload
/valleyshuttle.pdf

VISITOR CENTERS AND RANGER STATIONS

o Yosemite Valley Visitor Center and Bookstore: exhibits on
the Miwok and Paiute, the American Indian tribes native to
the area, and films about the area
o Yosemite Conservation Heritage Center
o Happy Isles Art and Nature Center

- Yosemite Valley Wilderness Center
- Tuolumne Meadows Wilderness Center
- Big Oak Flat Information Station
- Wawona Visitor Center at Hill's Studio
- Hetch Hetchy Entrance Station
- Badger Pass Ranger Station

BACKPACKING TRIP PLANNING

The Big Outside: www.thebigoutside.com

Contractors and Concessions

Aramark-Yosemite National Park, www.travelyosemite.com
Contact this authorized park concessionaire for reservations for all sorts of activities including biking, rafting, tours, and special events. Site is generally helpful for planning purposes.

Bicycle rentals in Yosemite Valley:
- Half Dome Village
- Yosemite Valley Lodge

Boat rentals in Yosemite Valley:
- Yosemite Valley Lodge Tour Desk
- Half Dome Village Tour and Activities Kiosk
- Yosemite Village Tour and Activities Kiosk
- The Majestic Yosemite Hotel Concierge Desk

Camping and lodging reservations:
- Recreation.gov: www.recreation.gov or 877-444-6777

Rock climbing classes:
- Yosemite Mountaineering School & Guide Service, 209-372-8344

East Side of the Park Services
- Lee Vining, leevining.com, 760-647-6629
- Inyo National Forest, www.fs.usda.gov/main/inyo/home

- Of Inyo's several ranger districts, Mono Lake, 760-647-3044, is the most pertinent to a Yosemite area visit. The Mono Basin Visitor Center, 760-647-6331, may also be of interest.

West Side Park Services

Stanislaus National Forest:
www.fs.usda.gov/main/stanislaus/home
Supervisor's Office, 19777 Greenley Road, Sonora, CA 95370

Other Helpful Information

- California Department of Fish and Wildlife (fishing permits): www.wildlife.ca.gov/Licensing/Fishing
- National Park Service, www.nps.gov/yose/planyourvisit /backpacking.htm
- Yosemite Hikes: www.yosemitehikes.com; private page maintained by Russ Cary

Breathtaking vistas mark the final stages of the climb to Clouds Rest.

INDEX

Photo by Kaden McAllister

ABOUT THE AUTHORS

Harley McAllister works as a project manager but feels most alive when he is outdoors, especially with his wife, Abby, and their children. He has lived in seven different states and on three different coasts, including four years with his family in the Dominican Republic teaching at a nonprofit school. Harley has rafted, skied, snorkeled, backpacked, mountain biked, and camped in diverse locations in both North and South America. He has spent a lot of time off the pavement and loves to share his passions with others to inspire them to get outside more often and have fun doing it.

Abby McAllister is a sometimes-harried mom of eight children, an outdoor enthusiast, a kitchen chemist, and a copycat crafter. Together, she and her husband, Harley, have traveled the world, always seeking opportunities to get their children out exploring nature. When she is not outside, she is busy writing books and blogs to help other people get their kids unplugged and outside.

Get more travel tips from the McAllisters' website: www.our4outdoors.com.

OTHER TITLES YOU MIGHT ENJOY FROM MOUNTAINEERS BOOKS

CAMPFIRE STORIES
Tales from America's National Parks

Dave Kyu and Ilyssa Kyu

Soak up tales from well-known writers, passages from pioneer diaries, and stories passed down through generations of indigenous peoples. Covers Acadia, Great Smoky, Rocky Mountain, Yellowstone, Yosemite, and Zion National Parks.

ADVENTURE HANDBOOK

Gav and Shell Grayston

Explore the great outdoors with your kids through the activities in this fun-filled guide.

100 CLASSIC HIKES: NORTHERN CALIFORNIA
Fourth Edition

John Soares

Enjoy a mother lode of outdoor treasures from Crescent City to Santa Cruz and east across the state in this lush, full-color guide.

YELLOWSTONE NATIONAL PARK:
Adventuring with Kids

Harley and Abby McAllister

The first volume in the Adventuring with Kids series is a guide to the world's first national park: Yellowstone National Park

www.mountaineersbooks.org